The Fearless Credit Professional

Credit Case Studies, Checklists and Credit Decision Frameworks

Kumar Gaurav Khullar

(Ex-Bank of India, Ex-Punjab & Sind Bank)

Made with ♥ on the Notion Press Platform

www.notionpress.com

To my mother, Smt. Punam,
you did not just bring me up, you built a life out of broken pieces and then handed it to me with dignity.
In every difficult decision I have ever taken, I have felt your quiet courage standing behind me like a wall.
If I have learned to stay steady when pressure rises, it is because I watched you do it first.

To my wife, Dr.Tanu,
you saw a writer and a teacher in me long before the world did.
When I hesitated, you gave me belief.
When I stepped away from certainty, you gave me stability.
This journey carries your fingerprint on every page and in every renewed attempt.

To my daughters, Pavi and Udyati,
you are my soft place to return to.
You turn fatigue into laughter and worry into calm.
If this book teaches strength, it is because you remind me daily that real strength can be gentle, playful, and full of love.

This book is not only dedicated to you.
It is powered by you.

CONTENTS

Preface

Dear fellow credit professionals,

A credit file rarely arrives with a warning label. It arrives with a neat proposal, a confident borrower, a healthy CIBIL score, a valuation report that looks reassuring, and a senior who needs an answer before end of day. Yet you know the truth: credit is not decided by what is visible. It is decided by what you question, verify, structure, and document. And when those steps are skipped, even once, the gap that follows can define a career in the worst possible way.

I wrote this book because most credit careers are not damaged by spectacular frauds. They are damaged by small, silent gaps that looked minor in the moment. A condition never complied with. A title comfort taken at face value. A charge creation step assumed to be done. A stock statement accepted without ageing discipline. Months later, when stress appears, those gaps become the centre of every uncomfortable question: *Why did you approve? What was your basis? What was your fallback?* This book exists so that you always have a confident, documented answer.

Where this journey began?

When I joined the bank as a Probationary Officer, I was posted directly to a Scale IV branch, carrying serious responsibility from day one. I had no mentor. Calls to the Zonal/Regional offices were politely deflected; they simply did not have time for a newbie's questions may be due to workload. Training college sessions were good but thorough on definitions and almost silent on practice. I asked friends in other branches/banks and heard the same story everywhere. We were all learning by making mistakes that, in hindsight, could have been avoided entirely if someone had simply walked us through one real case from start to finish.

That gap has not closed. Promotions have only accelerated since then. Young officers today reach positions of serious credit responsibility far earlier than their predecessors, often before they have seen enough varied files to build genuine instinct. After I wrote my previous book, *"The Fearless Banker"*, I began receiving one consistent request from credit officers, branch heads, and underwriters across the country: "*Write something only for credit. Show us real cases. Show us how to think.*" This book is my direct answer to that request.

What you will find inside?

The Fearless Credit Professional brings you twenty-three high-impact case studies built around the decisions that define a credit professional's reputation. Each case is written like a realistic file on your desk: the borrower narrative, the numbers, the security comfort, the gaps, the pressure, and the alternatives. You will see how a CIBIL score of 746 hid seventeen recent loan enquiries and a quietly settled old account. You will see how a fruit trader's round-tripping demolished an apparently strong working capital story. You will see how a ₹56-crore steel consortium unravelled when pari passu charge language was ambiguous and CERSAI filings were inconsistent, leading the lender straight to the DRT. You will see how a bullet gold loan backed by a wife's streedhan jewellery crossed the line into evergreening and how the bank caught it in time.

Training colleges will give you the definitions. This book will show you the decisions.

In practice, many sanction mistakes are actually process mistakes that surface much later. The best credit professionals think beyond the approval. They think about enforceability, recoverability, and how well their reasoning will hold up under scrutiny months down the line.

All cases are derived from real world lending environments. To protect confidentiality, details have been anonymised and reconstructed. Names, places, and identifying facts are changed while preserving the credit logic and the risk patterns.

Value you can use from day one

Beyond the case discussions, this book gives you tools you can apply at your desk immediately.

Many new credit professionals also fear the Personal Discussion(PD) with the borrowers. They sit across from a borrower and do not know what to ask, how to probe, or how to interpret what the borrower says and, equally importantly, what he carefully avoids saying. Several cases in this book walk you through

PD scenarios in depth: how to rebuild a kirana owner's real income from footfall and invoice reality, how to read a dhaba owner's cash flows when most transactions are cash-driven, how to spot a polished borrower hiding structural stress behind confident answers. By the time you finish this book, the PD will feel less like an interrogation you dread and more like a diagnostic tool you command.

To make every concept immediately actionable, the book also includes dedicated checklists for critical credit areas like: Power of Attorney, Bank Guarantee, Gold Loans, first versus Pari Passu versus Second Charge, Vehicle Loans, Pledge Finance, Stock Statement Analysis, GST-Based Credit Appraisal, Working Capital Loans, Personal Discussion, Hypothecation, and Loan Against Property. These are not generic checklists lifted from policy circulars. They are built directly from the mistakes, near-misses, and hard recoveries you will read about in the cases. Print them. Keep them at your desk. Use them before every sanction note you write.

Who should read this book?

This book is written for credit officers, branch credit in-charges, relationship managers, NBFC appraisal teams, and every officer who has been handed the advances desk, fully or partially, and is trying to do it well. If you are preparing for a promotion interview or Credit Manager's post interview, these cases will sharpen your applied thinking far beyond what any standard text can offer.

Let me say this clearly. If you study this book carefully, your probability of facing a show-cause notice, a disciplinary action, or a suspension over a credit decision drops sharply. Not because you will never face a difficult call; you will, every single week. But because you will make that call with your reasoning documented, your assumptions on record, and your sanction note written in a way that any senior, auditor, or vigilance officer can read, follow, and respect.

What "Fearless" means here?

"Fearless" does not mean aggressive lending. It means disciplined lending. It means knowing when to pause, what to verify, how to structure, and how to record your reasoning clearly. It means protecting the bank, serving the right borrowers, and standing firmly behind a well-documented yes or a well-documented no.

Remember, Credit is judged twice: on the day you sanction, and on the day someone reviews the file after a surprise event, a downturn, or a missed instalment. This book is written for your future self, the version of you who must answer tough questions with calm clarity.

You do not need a mentor looking over your shoulder anymore.

Open the first case. That is where we begin.

– Kumar Gaurav Khullar

CASE STUDY 1

POWER OF ATTORNEY IN LOAN TAKEOVER – WHEN A CONVENIENCE BECOMES A CREDIT RISK

How a PoA-based LAP takeover nearly exposed a bank to unsecured exposure on a high-value mortgage

1. Introduction

Shubham Cooperative Bank Ltd. (SCBL), a fast-growing private sector bank, had been aggressively canvassing Loan Against Property (LAP) takeovers to build its retail asset book. In many cases, especially where borrowers were NRIs or lived out of station, the bank relied on Power of Attorney (PoA) / Authorisation Deeds to complete closure with the existing lender and collect original title documents.

This case examines one such takeover proposal where the entire disbursement and mortgage creation depended on a PoA, raising critical questions around legal validity, stamping, registration, and operational risk for the credit team.

2. Borrower / Business Background

The proposed borrower, Mr. Rohan Lokhande, was an NRI software engineer working in Dubai. He owned a residential flat in Talegaon Dabhade, Maharashtra, which was currently mortgaged to Janta Housing Finance Ltd. (JHFL) against a LAP facility.

Key background:

- Original LAP with JHFL: ₹1 crore, sanctioned five years earlier.
- Current outstanding (as per JHFL foreclosure letter): ₹88 lakh.
- EMI track record: broadly regular with a few minor delays, but no SMA or NPA classification.
- Purpose of takeover: to reduce interest rate, shift relationship to SCBL, and obtain an additional top-up of ₹7 lakh for home renovation.

Since Mr. Lokhande was abroad, his younger brother Mr. Varun Lokhande, residing in Talegaon Dabhade, was coordinating with SCBL and a local DSA (Direct Selling Agent) for the takeover.

3. Facility Details

SCBL proposed the following facility, subject to due diligence and mortgage creation:

a) Facility type: Loan Against Property - Takeover + Top-up.

b) Amount: ₹95 lakh (₹88 lakh to close JHFL + ₹7 lakh top-up).

c) Tenure: 15 years.

d) Interest: Floating rate linked to SCBL's retail MCLR.

e) Security: (i)Equitable mortgage of the Talegaon Dabhade flat in Mr. Rohan Lokhande's name, (ii) Extension of charge for full ₹95 lakh.

f) Repayment: EMI from NRE savings account with SCBL.

Given the borrower's absence from India, the DSA informed the branch that a PoA executed abroad in favour of Mr. Varun Lokhande would be used for all documentation with both banks.

4. Scenario / Developments

The case moved quickly at first. SCBL completed financial appraisal based on salary slips, NRE statements, and copies of existing JHFL loan documents. The branch received a scanned copy of the PoA executed by Rohan in Dubai authorising Varun to deal with all banks and raise loans against property.

Caught between top management pressure to close the takeover and meet annual targets, and a false sense of comfort from an oral, unrecorded positive reply from the empanelled advocate (a combination that is a sure-shot recipe for bypassing due process), the branch:

- Logged in the proposal and obtained in-principle sanction.
- Prepared a Demand Draft of ₹88 lakh in favour of JHFL, with loan account number.
- Issued a covering letter authorising Varun, "as attorney of the borrower," to deliver the DD and collect all original property documents and NOC from JHFL.

When Varun visited JHFL's branch, their officials raised multiple objections:

i) They questioned his authority, stating they would normally hand over original title deeds only to the borrower or his properly documented attorney.

ii) They pointed out that the PoA copy produced was not registered with the local Sub-Registrar, and the original was stated to be in Dubai.

iii) They were unwilling to release documents without written confirmation from Rohan, directly addressed to them.

Simultaneously, SCBL's empanelled advocate, on deeply reviewing the scanned PoA, flagged issues around stamping, registration, and vague wording of powers for mortgage creation. He advised that the PoA, as it stood, was unsafe to rely upon for creating mortgage and executing loan documents.

Meanwhile, the DD was already issued in SCBL's books, and interest had started accruing, even though JHFL had not yet accepted the DD or closed their loan.

5. Problem Statement

a) Validity and enforceability of an overseas PoA that was inadequately stamped and not registered in India.

b) Ambiguous scope of powers, with no clear, transaction-specific authorisation to collect title deeds and create mortgage in favour of SCBL.

c) Operational and interest cost risk to SCBL arising from early issue of takeover DD before resolving PoA-related objections.

d) Inadequate documentation and internal noting of reliance on PoA and associated legal risks in the credit proposal and sanction terms.

e) Potential security risk if JHFL handed documents to the borrower's brother directly, with no clear obligation to lodge them with SCBL.

6. Detailed Analysis & Discussion

From a credit risk perspective, SCBL had correctly assessed income, repayment capacity, and overall LTV. The real vulnerability lay in security creation and process control, which were heavily dependent on the PoA.

The PoA executed by Rohan in Dubai was a broad, general PoA, allowing Varun to operate bank accounts and deal with property in general terms. It did not specifically mention the Talegaon Dabhade flat, the proposed SCBL LAP, or the closure of JHFL's account. From a legal standpoint, PoA powers are interpreted narrowly; an attorney cannot exceed the authority expressly granted.

Further, the PoA had only been notarised abroad. It had not been attested by the Indian Consulate, adjudicated in India, or registered with the jurisdictional Sub-Registrar, even though it related to dealings in immovable property. Under local stamp laws and practical banking norms, such a document is considered defective and cannot be safely relied upon to create a mortgage.

The advocate also pointed out that Power of Attorney does not transfer ownership; the Supreme Court's *Suraj Lamp & Industries Pvt Ltd. v/s State of Haryana (2011)* has clarified that GPA/PoA arrangements cannot substitute a registered sale deed for title. For banks, this means the mortgage must rest on the principal owner's valid title, not on the attorney's actions alone.

SCBL had also overlooked another critical safeguard recommended in many bank manuals: whenever a PoA is used for mortgage creation, the bank should directly confirm with the principal (Rohan) that: i) He has indeed executed the PoA, ii) It is still in force and not revoked, and iii) He has no objection to the attorney creating a mortgage in favour of the bank.

No such direct confirmation was obtained before issuing the DD. This weakness could later be exploited by the borrower to challenge the validity of the mortgage or to dispute Varun's actions.

Additionally, by issuing the DD upfront, SCBL exposed itself to:

a) Double interest risk - interest running in SCBL's books while JHFL had not yet closed the account; and

b) Process risk - if documents were delayed, lost, or withheld by JHFL or by the attorney, SCBL might be left with an unsecured exposure.

An internal review by the regional credit head observed that the sanction note did not explicitly document: Reliance on PoA, Need for special conditions, and requirement of a clear legal opinion on PoA sufficiency. This gap could attract criticism from auditors and vigilance authorities in case of future default.

7. Applicable Laws / Regulations

Several legal and regulatory aspects were relevant in this case:

a) **Powers of Attorney Act, 1882:** defines PoA as an instrument whereby one person authorises another to act on his behalf. The attorney's authority is limited to what is stated or necessarily implied in the document.

b) **State Stamp Act and Registration Act:** PoA dealing with immovable property often requires specific stamp duty and, in many states, **compulsory registration.** An unstamped or improperly stamped PoA may not be admissible in evidence and is unsafe for creating security.

c) **Suraj Lamp judgments of the Supreme Court:** clarify that GPA/PoA arrangements do not transfer title; banks must ensure that mortgage rests on valid ownership title, not on PoA-executed "sale-like" structures.

d) **KYC / AML directions and RBI's prudential norms:** require proper KYC of both principal and attorney, clear documentation, and enforceable security creation before recognising an advance as fully secured.

Failure to comply may not only weaken legal enforceability but can also lead to adverse classification in inspections.

Power of Attorney in Takeover Cases

A Power of Attorney (PoA) is a written authority allowing one person (attorney) to act on behalf of another (principal). In loan takeovers, PoA is often used when the borrower is an NRI or cannot be physically present to close the existing loan with the old bank, collect original title deeds, and execute fresh loan and mortgage documents with the new bank.

From a risk angle, banks should prefer a special PoA, which is limited to a specific property and transaction, clearly naming the new bank, old bank, and authorised actions. A general PoA with vague, broad powers is harder to control and easier to misuse.

Some banks also take an Authorisation / Indemnity Deed from the borrower, confirming that the bank's official is authorised to collect title deeds from the old bank and that any loss in the process will be borne by the borrower.

8. Outcome / Final Decision

After detailed deliberation, SCBL's regional credit committee decided not to proceed with the takeover on the existing PoA. Instead, they kept the sanction "in-principle" and imposed strict pre-disbursement conditions:

1) Rohan had to execute a fresh, special PoA in favour of Varun, specifically authorising:
    - Closure of the JHFL loan,
    - Collection of original title documents and NOC, and
    - Creation of mortgage and execution of all loan/security documents in favour of SCBL for the Talegaon Dabhade flat.
2) The new PoA had to be:
    - Properly stamped as per state law,
    - Attested by Indian Consulate abroad, and
    - Adjudicated and registered with the local Sub-Registrar in Talegaon Dabhade.
3) SCBL would issue the takeover DD only after:
    - Receiving the original registered PoA,
    - Favourable legal opinion specifically certifying PoA sufficiency, and
    - Obtaining a direct email/letter from Rohan confirming that the PoA is subsisting and not revoked.

Pending these, the earlier DD was cancelled and reversed in the system to avoid unnecessary interest load.

Eventually, Rohan complied with the conditions, the new PoA was registered, JHFL released all original documents against SCBL's DD to the authorised official, and a valid equitable mortgage was created in favour of SCBL. The account has since been conducted satisfactorily.

9. Key Lessons for Credit Professionals

a) Never rely on a PoA for mortgage creation or document collection unless it is properly stamped, registered (where required), and legally vetted for that specific property and transaction.

b) Insist on a special, transaction-specific PoA for takeover cases, clearly authorising closure of the old loan, collection of title deeds, and creation of security in favour of your bank.

c) Document in the sanction note that the bank is relying on PoA, and make legal opinion and direct confirmation from the principal pre-disbursement conditions.

d) Avoid issuing takeover DDs or initiating disbursement before all PoA-related doubts are resolved; otherwise, the bank may face double interest and unsecured exposure risk.

e) Treat PoA as a controlled exception tool, not a routine convenience. Borrower presence should remain the default, especially in high-value LAP and property-backed exposures.

PoA Checklist for Credit Professional's and Underwriter's learnings

1. Always verify that the name on the title documents and sanction letters matches the principal borrower, and not merely the attorney who is signing under the PoA.
2. Before relying on any PoA, check that it is properly executed, stamped, and (where required) registered in the same state where the mortgaged property is situated.
3. In NRI cases, accept a PoA for property or loan creation only if it bears appropriate consular attestation abroad and has been duly adjudicated on stamp duty in India.
4. Review the PoA text line by line to confirm that it specifically authorises the attorney to collect original title deeds, sign loan documents, and create mortgage/charge with banks and housing authorities.
5. Where the PoA is several years old, obtain a fresh written confirmation from the principal that it has not been revoked and that they ratify its use for the current loan transaction.
6. Ensure that the PoA empowers the attorney to appear before the Sub-Registrar and sign any required mortgage or MODTD (Memorandum of Deposit of Title Deeds) registration documents on behalf of the principal.

7. In housing society or development authority cases, check that the PoA includes authority to sign transfer forms, NOCs, and mutation/charge-creation documents wherever required.
8. Treat any PoA that contains very wide, generic powers to borrow any amount from any bank and create security as a red flag, and seek a narrowed, transaction-specific replacement.
9. For corporate or partnership borrowers, prefer board/partner resolutions and authorised signatories over PoA structures, using PoA only where there is a clear and documented necessity.
10. When using PoA in loan takeovers, always support it with a separate borrower authorisation/indemnity letter empowering the bank's official to collect documents from the existing lender and indemnifying the bank for that act.
11. Insist that the original registered PoA is produced for physical inspection at least once, and keep a clear, legible scanned copy in the credit file for future legal and audit reference.
12. Before disbursement, cross-verify that the PoA details (names, property description, powers granted) are consistent across the legal opinion, valuation report, and sanction note.
13. Do not permit any attorney to negotiate or receive disbursement proceeds directly into their own account; all funds must flow only to the principal's designated account as per sanction terms.
14. Where property has come through a GPA/PoA sale chain, obtain a specific legal opinion on marketable title and ensure that the bank is not indirectly relying on an impermissible "GPA sale" structure.
15. Record in the pre-disbursement checklist that the PoA has been vetted for authenticity (signatures, witnesses, identification of parties) and that KYC of both principal and attorney is complete.
16. Train branch and credit staff to escalate any doubt on PoA wording, stamping, jurisdiction, or age to the legal department instead of informally "adjusting" processes at the counter or DSA level.

•••

CASE STUDY 2

WHEN A "PERFECT" LAP PROPERTY STARTS CRACKING UNDER TECHNICAL SCRUTINY

1. Introduction

Assam Commercial Bank's Jorhat Branch in East India had been aggressively growing its secured retail book through Loan Against Property (LAP). Delinquency was low, competition was intense, and business teams were under pressure to log clean cases backed by apparently strong residential properties.

In this context, a LAP proposal reached the Credit Manager's table. The borrower's CIBIL was good, income was stable, and the property value seemed more than adequate. However, once the technical report was read line-by-line and cross-verified with independent field checks, the "perfect" collateral turned into a borderline case.

This case study walks through how a technically acceptable report, if not critically analysed, could have exposed the bank to serious enforceability and marketability risk.

2. Borrower & Business Background

The borrower, **Mr. Arjun Gogoi (42)**, is proprietor of **Gogoi Agro Distributors**, a semi-urban fertiliser and seeds distributor operating for the last eight years in Jorhat, a city in East India.

Key profile points (as per application and financials):

- Vintage: 8 years in the same line of business.
- Turnover: Around ₹1.8 crore in the latest year, with moderate seasonality.
- Profitability: Net profit margin around 6 - 7%.
- Existing Limits: Small CC limit of ₹10 lakh from Assam Commercial Bank; account standard with satisfactory conduct.
- Existing Borrowings: Two unsecured business loans of ₹8 lakh each from NBFCs at high interest rates.

The borrower is viewed as a typical lower - mid ticket SME customer: reasonable cash flows, but limited financial sophistication and a tendency to use high-cost NBFC loans for quick liquidity.

3. Facility Proposal & Security Offered

Mr. Gogoi applied for a LAP Term Loan of ₹35 lakh for:

- Consolidation of high-cost NBFC loans
- Additional working capital for stocking during peak agricultural season

Key proposal parameters:

- Product: Loan Against Property - Term Loan.
- Tenor: 10 years.
- Repayment: EMI from business income.
- Primary Security: Equitable mortgage of self-owned residential house located in Village Rangamati, near Jorhat, approximately 40 km from the branch.
- Property Status: Independent residential house in a gram panchayat area, claimed to be fully constructed and self-occupied.

On the face of it, LTV appeared comfortable based on the initial technical summary, and FOIR (Fixed Obligation to Income Ratio) was within internal norms.

4. Technical Valuation Report - As Actually Received by the Credit Manager

4.1 Valuation / Technical Report - Residential House (For LAP)

Client: Assam Commercial Bank - Jorhat Branch.

Product: Loan Against Property (LAP) - Term Loan.

Applicant: Mr. Arjun Gogoi (Co-applicant: Mrs. Kavita Gogoi).

Property Type: Independent Residential House.

Local Body: Gram Panchayat – Rangamati.

Date of Site Visit: 07.08.2025

Date of Report: 09.08.2025

Purpose of valuation: To assess fair market value, distress/realizable value and guideline value of the property offered as security against proposed LAP facility.

4.2 Property Identification & Location

Address as per documents: Residential house situated at Village Rangamati, Part of Survey No. 500, Gram Panchayat Rangamati, District Jorhat, East India; bounded as per sale deed.

Address as per actual site: House located in Rangamati Extension, near Government Girls School, approx. 40 km from Jorhat, East India.

GPS Coordinates (on site):

- Latitude: 23.826456
- Longitude: 77.946878

Access & Approach:

12-15 feet wide motorable village road abutting the plot on the eastern side; approach suitable for two-wheelers and small four-wheelers.

Distance from Key Points (approx.):

Bus stand: 3 - 4 km

Railway station: 8 - 10 km

Nearest town (Jorhat): 35 - 40 km

4.3 Four-Side Boundaries

As per sale deed:

East - Village road

West - House of Mr. S. Sharma

North - Open land

South - House of Mr. R. Das

As per site inspection:

East - Village road (same as deed).

West - House of Mr. S. Sharma (same as deed).

North - Partly constructed godown (new development in place of earlier open land).

South - House of Mr. R. Das (same as deed).

Valuer's remark: "Plot identified on the basis of sale deed description and local enquiry. Minor change in northern boundary due to subsequent construction; however, ownership and location of plot match document description."

4.4 Ownership & Occupation

Owner as per sale deed: Mrs. Kavita Gogoi, wife of Mr. Arjun Gogoi.

Nature of title: Freehold property, acquired by registered sale deed executed and registered in 2024 at Sub-Registrar Office, Jorhat.

Occupancy status: Self-occupied family residence; front portion used as small agro-input shop/godown and rear portion used for residential purpose.

Utilities & name verification:

- Electricity connection present; latest bill produced in the name of Mr. Ramesh Gogoi (father of applicant).
- Water connection available through village supply and borewell.

Valuer's remark: "Property in physical possession of Gogoi family. Electricity bill name differs from sale deed holder; relationship to be verified by bank/ legal team."

4.5 Property Description - Construction & Locality

a) **Locality class:** Predominantly lower - middle and middle-class residential; mixed use with small shops along main road.

b) **Habitation / development within 1 km:** Approx. 50% developed; presence of houses, small shops, school and basic amenities.

c) **Building nature:** Residential house with partial commercial use (front shop).

d) **Structure type:** Load-bearing, girder - Farsi type with brick masonry walls and flat roof.

e) **Year of construction:** Approx. 2015 (as informed and observed).

f) **Age & residual life:** About 10 years old; estimated residual economic life 40 - 45 years, assuming normal maintenance.

g) **Structural condition:** Overall average; minor dampness and hairline cracks noticed; no major structural distress observed at time of visit.

4.6 Area Statement

Land/plot area as per documents: 4,818 sq. ft.

Measured land/plot area at site: 4,752 sq. ft. (approx.)

Valuer's remark: "Some variation between deed area and site-measured area due to boundary alignment and measurement method. For valuation, lower area of 4,752 sq. ft. considered as a conservative measure."

Built-up area (ground floor only): 2,369 sq. ft. (includes rooms, kitchen, hall, shop portion and verandah).

Carpet area (internal usable): Approx. 2,013 sq. ft. (estimated from built-up less walls and verandah).

4.7 Valuation –

Rates adopted (based on local enquiry and comparable properties):

- Land rate: ₹700 per sq. ft.
- Construction rate: ₹300 per sq. ft. for load-bearing structure of average quality.

Valuation workings:

Land value (4,752 sq. ft. × ₹700) = ₹33.26 lakh.

Construction value (2,369 sq. ft. × ₹300) = ₹7.11 lakh.

Total market value (rounded) = ₹40.37 lakh.

Distress / Realisable value (80% of market value) = ₹32.29 lakh

Government guideline (circle) rate: Approx. ₹418 per sq. ft. for land in this area, as per latest available records.

Valuer's note: "Prevailing market transactions are generally higher than guideline rate; adopted land rate of ₹700 per sq. ft. is in line with recent unregistered/registered deals as per broker feedback and local enquiry."

4.8 Compliance, Approvals & Deviations

a) **RERA applicability:** Not applicable - gram panchayat property, not part of notified RERA project.

b) **Building plan / sanction:** No sanctioned building plan or permission letter provided.

c) **Layout plan / occupancy certificate:** Not available; typical for gram panchayat area.

Valuer's remark: "No major structural or technical deviations observed at site compared to existing structure. However, building approvals and layout/occupancy certificates have not been furnished; bank may take appropriate legal opinion as per policy."

4.9 Additional Technical Observations

a) Property falls within a semi-rural belt with partly developed surroundings; marketability considered moderate.

b) Approach road is motorable but not very wide; large commercial vehicles may face difficulty turning near the property.

c) No evidence of major encroachment observed on visit date.

d) No high-tension line directly over the structure; alignment observed at a distance beyond property boundary (exact clearance to be considered as per bank norms).

4.10 Overall Technical Opinion (As Stated by Valuer)

"Considering location, access, development level, construction quality and prevailing market conditions, the subject property is technically acceptable and suitable as collateral security for the proposed LAP facility, subject to satisfactory legal scrutiny of title, family/ownership aspects and bank's internal policy regarding gram panchayat properties and absence of approved building plan."

5. Key Developments

The Sales Manager had already logged the case, collected property chain documents and initiated legal and technical reports. Convinced by the high valuation, he repeatedly highlighted that the collateral "more than covers" the requested facility.

When the technical report reached the Credit Manager, instead of just glancing at the summary, he applied an internal technical checklist covering:

- Property identification, address matching, GPS verification.
- Ownership and title clarity.
- Construction stage, area, and deviations.
- Approach road, location, habitation level.
- Valuation reasonableness.
- Photographs, legal red flags and independent site checks.

He also used an additional on-site risk check list focusing on distance from railway tracks and high-tension lines, proximity to water bodies, approach-road width, zoning, property usage, structural safety, occupancy, utilities and proximity to dumping yards or cremation sites.

Based on these tools, he called for an independent visit accompanied by the Sales Manager. What they found altered the entire risk assessment.

6. Problem Statement

a) Property identification and boundary mismatches created doubt on enforceability.

b) Ownership, utility-bill names and actual usage raised title and declaration concerns.

c) Area discrepancies and valuation assumptions made LTV comfort questionable.

d) Absence of formal approvals and unclear zoning increased legal and regulatory risk.

e) External technical risks (railway track, HT line, water body, low habitation) undermined marketability in a stress scenario.

7. Detailed Analysis

7.1 Property Identification & Boundary Mismatches

The report contained two addresses - one "as per documents" and one "as per site". While broadly similar, the on-site board showed the locality name as "Rangamati Extension" whereas the sale deed mentioned "Rangamati Village". The valuer had correctly recorded both variants.

Four-side boundaries in the sale deed mentioned:

East - Village road

West - Neighbour's house (Mr. S. Sharma)

North - Open land

South - House of Mr. R. Das

However, at site, the north side had a partly constructed godown owned by an unrelated party. The valuer had noted this change in the remarks, but the Sales team had not flagged it.

In isolation, such changes might be acceptable (given time gap and local development), provided the valuer clearly confirms that the plot measured and the plot in the deed are the same. But the combination of minor address variation and boundary change made the Credit Manager uncomfortable, as any ambiguity here could be exploited during SARFAESI enforcement or sale in auction.

7.2 Ownership, Utility-Bill Names & Actual Usage

The sale deed showed the owner as Mrs. Kavita Gogoi, wife of Mr. Arjun Gogoi, with Mr. Gogoi as co-applicant in the LAP. On site, however:

- Electricity bills were in the name of Mr. Ramesh Gogoi, the borrower's father.
- The nameplate on the property displayed "R. Gogoi & Sons".
- The front portion of the house was being used as a small agro-input shop and godown, while the rear portion was residential.

The valuer had correctly recorded that an electricity meter was installed, that bills were available but in a different name, and that local enquiry confirmed ownership by the Gogoi family.

From a credit-risk perspective, the issues were:

a) Title appeared to be family-based and not entirely ring-fenced around the main applicant and co-applicant.

b) Actual use was mixed (commercial + residential), while the proposal declared it purely as a residential self-occupied house; this mismatch could affect both internal policy classification and enforceability of security.

c) Legal opinion would have to clearly address the effect of family rights, ancestral nature (if any), and whether the mortgage could be validly created without challenge.

7.3 Area & Valuation Concerns - Is the LTV Really Comfortable?

The report noted a difference between document area (4,818 sq. ft.) and measured area (4,752 sq. ft.), and correctly valued only the lower area.

On deeper discussion with the valuer, the Credit Manager found:

- The land rate of ₹700 per sq. ft. was based on two recent but unregistered local transactions reported verbally by brokers.
- Official guideline rate (circle rate) was around ₹418 per sq. ft., implying the valuation rate used was significantly higher than guideline, though not necessarily unrealistic for prevailing market.
- Construction quality was average load-bearing type; yet, ₹300 per sq. ft. was used uniformly, without any discount for visible dampness at the rear and minor cracks on the side wall.

Given the requested LAP of ₹35 lakh, a casual reader might say: "Market value is ₹40.4 lakh, distress value is around ₹32.3 lakh - overall okay." But from a risk manager's lens:

- If forced-sale realisation in this semi-rural location is assumed at 60 - 65% of market value and not the assumed 80%, actual realisable value could be materially lower.
- Any legal or technical imperfection further reduces the bidder universe in auction, making recovery uncertain.

Thus, the apparent LTV comfort started looking fragile once assumptions were questioned.

7.4 Approvals, Zoning & Regulatory Concerns

The property was in a gram panchayat area. The technical report clearly mentioned:

- No sanctioned building plan submitted.
- No building-permission letter.
- No occupancy certificate.
- No formal conversion document evidencing change from agricultural to residential status.

These omissions are common in village properties, but they create a serious policy question: can such properties be treated as standard residential collateral, or only as "additional" collateral with capped valuation?

From a regulatory angle, RBI does not prohibit lending against such properties; however, it expects banks to have robust board-approved policies, ensure enforceability of security and avoid technical defects that can delay or derail SARFAESI enforcement in default. Lack of clear zoning and approvals increases the risk of legal challenge from local authorities or neighbours at the time of enforcement.

In this case, the bank's internal policy permitted gram panchayat properties only if:

- There was clear documentary evidence of construction being in existence for a minimum number of years, and
- Legal opinion confirmed that the mortgage was enforceable and the structure was not in violation of any notified land use.

The absence of formal approvals made the case policy-sensitive and dependent on a strong legal report.

7.5 External Technical Risks & Marketability

Using the additional field-check list, the Credit Manager and Sales Manager observed:

a) A railway track around 250 - 270 metres from the property, slightly below the internal comfort guideline of 300 metres.

b) A high-tension electricity line running parallel to the rear boundary at an estimated horizontal distance of about 15 metres - just at the minimum threshold; any measurement error could put it below.

c) A seasonal nala (water channel) approximately 70 - 80 metres away. In heavy monsoon years, locals reported waterlogging in low-lying plots closer to the nala.

d) Habitation level in the 1 km radius was around 35 - 40%, lower than the bank's preferred 40%+ for comfortable marketability.

Individually, some of these factors could be tolerated with conditions. However, when combined with address/boundary variations, ownership complications and lack of approvals, the property began to look marginal rather than strong collateral.

8. Outcome / Final Credit Decision

The proposal was placed before the Branch Credit Committee (with regional credit participation) with a detailed note highlighting:

- **Business strengths:** reasonable financials, standard conduct in existing CC account, genuine business need, satisfactory CIBIL profile.
- **Collateral concerns:** identification mismatches, ownership and usage issues, aggressive valuation assumptions, lack of approvals, and external technical risks affecting marketability.

After discussion, the committee concluded:

a) The credit worthiness of Mr. Gogoi was acceptable for a moderate LAP ticket, and his intention appeared genuine.

b) However, the offered property could not be treated as a strong primary security due to cumulative technical and legal risks.

c) In a SARFAESI or auction scenario, any dispute on boundaries, family ownership, unauthorised construction or proximity to HT line/railway track could materially depress recovery, especially in a semi-rural market.

Final Decision:

a) The LAP proposal of ₹35 lakh was declined in its present form.

b) The borrower was advised that the bank could reconsider a secured facility if:
   - He offered an alternate technically compliant property with clear approvals and zoning, or
   - He accepted a significantly lower limit backed by this property only as additional collateral, post strong legal vetting and with conservative valuation.

The decision was recorded with detailed reasoning to protect the bank and the officers from future audit or vigilance queries, given that the case could easily have been sanctioned if the technical report had been read superficially.

9. Key Lessons for Credit Professionals

a) Never rely only on the valuation summary - always read the full technical report, including address versions, boundaries, remarks and photographs.

b) LTV comfort is an illusion if valuation assumptions (area, rate, distress factor) are aggressive or unsupported by documentary and market evidence.

c) Ownership, utility-bill names, actual usage (residential vs mixed/ commercial) and absence of approvals can together weaken enforceability, even when the legal title initially appears clear.

d) External technical risks - railway tracks, HT lines, water bodies, low habitation and narrow approach roads - directly impact future saleability and must be factored into credit decisions.

e) Regulatory expectation is not just to create a mortgage, but to ensure that collateral is realistically realisable; credit officers must boldly decline or restructure deals where technical risk outweighs business pressure.

LAP Checklist for Credit Professionals

1. LAP eligibility is income and P&L driven, so compute FOIR rigorously before taking comfort from property value.
2. Cap LTV tightly, typically 65–70% for residential, and reduce further for commercial, industrial, or plot assets due to weaker liquidity.
3. Underwrite the assumption that borrower income will remain stable for 10–15 years, because margin in property cannot compensate for a weak repayment story.
4. Keep FOIR broadly within 55–65% of gross income to preserve cushion for household expenses, emergencies, and volatility.
5. Use DSCR to validate business viability but use FOIR to validate household repayment capacity, and never substitute one for the other.
6. In MSME-backed LAP, test true earning capacity through market visits, reference checks, lifestyle indicators, and banking pattern analysis, not only books.
7. Apply the matching concept strictly so every income considered in eligibility has its linked obligation captured in FOIR.
8. Accept only fixed and continuous income for LAP, and exclude one-time gains, speculative profits, irregular dividends, or windfalls without exception.
9. Treat future obligations currently in pre-EMI or moratorium as full EMI in FOIR because the LAP runs long after the moratorium ends.
10. If EMI details are not available, compute obligations using conservative product-appropriate assumptions on tenor and ROI instead of ignoring liabilities.

11. Obtain final valuation only from the empanelled technical channel and ensure internal approval before disbursement, because credit owns LTV compliance.
12. Read the full technical report including boundaries, photographs, construction quality, deviations, and remarks, because headline market value can be misleading.
13. Reject securities where access, approvals, or external risks materially damage enforceability and saleability, even if LTV appears comfortable.
14. Obtain legal title search only from an empanelled advocate and comply with every remark before releasing any disbursement.
15. Confirm chain of title, link documents, mutation flow, and clear encumbrance status so ownership and mortgage rights are litigation-resistant.
16. Ensure all owners and necessary family stakeholders are appropriately bound in the structure as per policy to avoid consent and enforcement gaps later.
17. Do not allow tenancy creation in mortgaged property without prior written bank approval, because possession becomes materially harder during default.
18. If property is already tenanted, insist on a strong lease with a clear vacation clause and obtain tenant undertaking where enforceability is weak.
19. Fix a non-negotiable timeline for equitable mortgage creation and MODT (Memorandum of Deposit of Title Deeds) formalities, and obtain a fitment certificate after originals are received.
20. In takeover cases, verify completeness of originals against the advocate checklist and do not rely on scanned sets for final comfort.
21. Treat Power of Attorney cases as higher risk and rely only on transaction-specific, stamped, and registered POA with explicitly verified powers.
22. Mandate building insurance for full reinstatement value with bank clause endorsement within specified timelines, and treat failure to renew annually within due date as a non-compliance triggering corrective action.
23. Verify approvals and compliance status such as sanctioned plan, completion or occupancy evidence, and tax-payment continuity to avoid hidden legal friction.

24. Compute DSCR using sustainable operating profit by removing one-time incomes and personal withdrawals so cash flow reflects long-term reality.
25. Keep charge creation and security documentation updated, including CERSAI and ROC wherever applicable, especially after enhancements or facility additions.
26. In family-pooled LAP structures, map each co-applicant's income against their own obligations first, and only then combine net surpluses.
27. Treat any EMI bounce or irregular account conduct as a red flag requiring a comprehensive reassessment of cash flows, loan terms and conditions, and collateral risk, rather than merely a routine payment follow-up.

•••

CASE STUDY 3

WHEN A "GOOD" CIBIL SCORE MASKS A WEAK CREDIT STORY

Why experienced credit officers never underwrite unsecured loans on score alone

1. Introduction

Sahyog Small Finance Bank, a mid-sized private sector bank, had set ambitious targets for high-ticket personal loans in its urban branches. One such branch in Bengaluru received an attractive proposal: a self-employed services professional seeking a ₹35 lakh unsecured personal loan for "business expansion and consolidation of high-cost borrowings".

The CIBIL score was 746 which was comfortably above the bank's internal minimum threshold of 720 for unsecured retail exposures. The branch was keen to book the asset quickly.

However, the credit team believed in one core principle: *"CIBIL score is only a filter, not the final decision. The real story lies in the patterns and remarks."*

This case captures how multiple moderate red flags in the CIBIL report when looked at together can significantly alter the risk perception in a seemingly "acceptable" personal loan proposal.

2. Borrower Profile & Business Background

Borrower: Mr. Arjun Mehta, 39 years, married, residing in a self-owned flat in Bengaluru.

Profile: Arjun is a self-employed management consultant, primarily advising mid-sized businesses on marketing and process improvement.

Business vintage: 7 years (proprietorship concern: Mehta Consulting Services).

Declared annual gross receipts (latest FY): ₹60 lakh.

Declared profit after tax (average of last 3 years): around ₹28–30 lakh.

Average monthly credits in main current account (last 12 months): around ₹5.0–5.5 lakh.

The spouse is employed in an IT company, but the proposed loan is in Arjun's single name. The branch informally considers the comfort of the household income, but as per the bank's retail credit policy, repayment capacity must be primarily assessed on the borrower's own documented income for unsecured loans.

Arjun maintains multiple banking relationships and has been a long-standing customer of Sahyog Small Finance Bank for savings and current accounts, but this is his first borrowing request with the bank.

3. Loan Proposal – Facility Details

Facility Type: Unsecured Personal Loan (term loan).

Proposed Limit: ₹35 lakh.

Purpose: Partly to expand his consulting practice (setting up a small office, hiring two staff) and partly to consolidate existing high-cost personal loans and credit card dues.

Key Terms (as per proposal):

Tenor: 60 months.

Proposed ROI: 14.25% p.a. fixed.

Approximate EMI: ₹81,500 per month.

Security: Clean (no collateral, only standard documentation and personal guarantee of borrower).

As per the bank's Board-approved retail credit policy and RBI's guidelines on unsecured retail lending, personal loans of this size require:

- CIBIL score ≥ 720.
- Satisfactory track record of existing borrowings.
- Acceptable FOIR (Fixed Obligations to Income Ratio).
- Clean or explainable CIBIL with no recent write-offs/settlements.

The branch, after reviewing ITRs, bank statements and net worth, found the profile "premium" and prepared a positive note, relying heavily on the high score.

4. CIBIL Report – Snapshot

The credit officer obtained Arjun's CIBIL report. Key highlights of the CIBIL report were:

CIBIL Score: 746.

Total accounts: 12 (8 closed, 4 active).

Active major facilities:

a) Home loan with a large private bank: outstanding around ₹48 lakh, EMI - ₹38,000.

b) Car loan with an NBFC: outstanding around ₹5 lakh, EMI - ₹12,000.

c) Existing personal loan with a fintech NBFC (equipment + personal use): outstanding approx. ₹9 lakh, EMI - ₹22,000.

d) Credit card with a limit of ₹3 lakh; last 6 months utilisation mostly between ₹2.6 - 2.9 lakh.

Past behaviour:

- One credit card written-off and settled account from 2016 (₹18,000 principal, partly written off).
- On the current personal loan, multiple 30 DPD and one 60 DPD in the last 24 months, regularised thereafter.

Enquiries: 17 enquiries in the last 9 months, predominantly for personal loans and top-ups in the range of ₹15 - 40 lakh.

Guarantor role: Guarantor to a ₹22 lakh term loan of "Mehta Logistics", a cousin's transport business with another bank, which has been in SMA-1 status twice in the last year.

Small-ticket loans: Two app-based micro personal loans (₹25,000 and ₹30,000 each) taken and closed within 3 - 4 months in the last year.

Addresses: Two residential addresses in different parts of the same city, consistent with his shift from rented accommodation to owned flat (validated with KYC).

On the face of it, there were no current overdues and the score was above the threshold. Yet, the patterns raised questions.

5. Problem Statement

a) Is it prudent to sanction a ₹35 lakh unsecured personal loan when the borrower already has multiple ongoing EMIs and a borderline FOIR?

b) How should the nine-year-old written-off and settled credit card be interpreted in today's credit decision, especially for an unsecured high-ticket loan?

c) Do 17 recent personal loan enquiries signal unacceptable "credit hunger" and liquidity stress, or can they be treated as normal loan shopping by a higher-income borrower?

d) What is the real risk impact of Arjun's guarantor exposure to Mehta Logistics' term loan, given its past SMA-1 behaviour?

e) Do the patterns of small app-based loans, high credit card utilisation and repeated short delinquencies indicate persistent liquidity management issues that could affect future repayment capacity?

6. Detailed Analysis

6.1. Score vs Behaviour –

The branch's first argument was simple: "Score is 746, well above grid requirements; there are no current overdues. We should proceed."

The credit officer looked deeper. The score was indeed strong, but the report also highlighted:

- A prior written-off/settled credit card.
- Repeated DPD instances on the ongoing personal loan.
- High utilisation on unsecured lines.
- Multiple recent enquiries for fresh unsecured credit.

In line with best practices, the credit officer treated the score as a screening tool, not a decision tool, focusing instead on repayment discipline and behavioural patterns over time.

6.2. Old Settlement - How Much Weight Should It Carry?

The 2016 credit card account was marked as "Written Off - Settled", with around ₹9,000 written off. Though nearly nine years old, this entry indicated that Arjun had previously negotiated to pay less than the full dues.

From a risk perspective, even small settlements:

- Question repayment intent during past stress.
- Show that when under pressure, the borrower chose settlement over full honouring of obligations.

The bank's policy did not impose an absolute bar on customers with old settlements older than five years, especially where overall conduct had improved. However, it required heightened scrutiny and risk-based pricing for unsecured exposures above ₹20 lakh.

The credit officer concluded - The old settlement is not an automatic rejection trigger, but it is a permanent caution flag that pushes this case out of the "low-risk" bucket.

6.3. Enquiry Behaviour - Credit Hunger or Logical Shopping?

17 enquiries in 9 months, mostly for personal loans between ₹15 - 40 lakh, were a clear indicator that Arjun was actively trying to raise additional unsecured funding.

Two interpretations were possible:

i) **Benign view (branch):** A financially literate borrower comparing offers across lenders; high-income profiles often explore multiple options.

ii) **Risk view (credit officer):** Combined with high card utilisation, small-ticket loans and existing EMIs, the pattern suggests liquidity pressure and attempts to plug gaps through unsecured borrowings.

The credit officer leaned towards the second interpretation, especially because only one of these enquiries translated into an actual live personal loan (the current NBFC loan). This raised the possibility that other lenders may have declined or reduced exposure based on their internal assessments.

6.4. Repayment Behaviour - Small but Repeated Slippages

The existing personal loan showed multiple 30 DPD and one 60 DPD instance in the last two years. Each delay was eventually regularised and the account never became NPA, but the pattern was telling:

- DPDs coinciding with periods of high card utilisation and micro-loan borrowings

- EMI bouncing and being cleared after a few days, indicating tight liquidity rather than pure oversight

From a prudential perspective, while RBI allows SMA and DPD slippages without automatic NPA classification, credit discipline over time is a behavioural risk indicator. Multiple minor slippages suggest that Arjun tends to stretch obligations during cash-flow tightness rather than maintain buffer. For a large unsecured personal loan, this is a serious behavioural risk.

6.5. Over-Utilisation and Micro-Loans - Liquidity Stress Signals

Arjun's main credit card utilisation was above 85 - 95% of limit for most months. In parallel, he had taken two app-based micro personal loans of ₹25,000 and ₹30,000, revolving them for a few months before closure.

Individually, these may look small. Collectively, they show:

- Dependence on high-cost, short-term credit.
- Limited internal liquidity buffer despite healthy declared income.
- A pattern of "patchwork" cash management.

From a risk perspective, this creates discomfort: when business receipts slow down or a major client delays payment, Arjun appears to rely on short-term loans and high card utilisation instead of using reserves.

6.6. Guarantor Exposure - A Silent Contingent Risk

Arjun is a personal guarantor for his cousin's company, Mehta Logistics, which enjoys a ₹22 lakh term loan from another bank. The CIBIL commercial section and guarantor mapping showed that this loan had slipped into SMA-1 twice in the last 12 months, before being regularised.

As per RBI norms and legal principles, a guarantor is co-extensively liable with the principal borrower. If Mehta Logistics were to ultimately default, the lender could invoke Arjun's guarantee and proceed against his personal assets and income.

For Sahyog Small Finance Bank, this translated into a contingent liability and correlation risk:

- Any serious stress in Mehta Logistics would directly impact Arjun's financial position.

- This risk is not reflected in his existing EMIs, but can crystallise suddenly.

The credit officer therefore treated the guarantor exposure as a hidden but material risk, further weakening the case for a large unsecured loan.

6.7. FOIR and Leverage - The Final Quantitative Check

Based on ITRs and income assessment, the credit officer considered Arjun's net monthly income at around ₹2.5 lakh (conservatively, ignoring spouse income for underwriting).

Existing EMIs:

- Home loan: ₹38,000.
- Car loan: ₹12,000.
- Current NBFC personal loan: ₹22,000.
- Total existing EMIs: ₹72,000.

If the new personal loan of ₹35 lakh with EMI of ₹81,500 was sanctioned, the total EMI burden would become around ₹1,53,500 per month. Resulting in FOIR of around 61% of net monthly income.

The internal policy preferred FOIR less than 55% for high-value unsecured loans, even for higher income brackets. With FOIR at 61%, coupled with behavioural red flags, the case moved from "borderline acceptable" to "highly stretched".

7. Outcome / Final Credit Decision

After deliberation, the Credit Committee decided on a calibrated middle path:

a) Sanction reduced personal loan of ₹20 lakh instead of ₹35 lakh.

b) Tenor retained at 60 months, with EMI of approximately ₹46,500.

c) With this reduced EMI, total EMI outgo becomes around ₹1,18,500, bringing FOIR closer to 47 - 48%, within acceptable internal limits.

d) Risk-based pricing: ROI increased by 50 bps (to 14.75% p.a.) to reflect higher behavioural and contingent risk.

e) Specific pre-conditions:

    - Arjun must close both app-based micro-loans (if any re-opened) and provide proof.

- He must reduce his card utilisation to below 50% of limit and avoid revolving large balances; this to be confirmed via latest statements.
- No further unsecured personal loans to be availed during the currency of this facility without prior written consent of Sahyog Bank.
- Quarterly monitoring of CIBIL for the first two years, with the account to be flagged as a "behavioural watch-list" borrower.

f) Arjun was counselled on the implications of his guarantor role for Mehta Logistics; the bank documented this in the credit note to ensure that future deterioration of that account would trigger a review.

This approach balanced business opportunity with prudence, reflecting RBI's expectations on responsible lending and internal risk-based pricing practices.

8. Key Lessons for Credit Professionals

a) **Never rely on score alone:** A high CIBIL score must be treated as a filter, not a decision; always read remarks, history, and behavioural patterns before underwriting.

b) **Treat settlements and write-offs as permanent caution marks:** Even small or old settled/written-off accounts should shift the case from "low-risk" to "heightened scrutiny", especially for unsecured loans.

c) **Analyse enquiry clusters and utilisation together:** Multiple recent personal loan enquiries, high credit card utilisation and small short-term loans, taken together, are strong indicators of credit hunger and liquidity stress.

d) **Factor guarantor exposures into overall risk:** A borrower who is guarantor to stressed or SMA-prone accounts carries hidden contingent risk that can suddenly impact repayment capacity and must be explicitly recorded in the credit note.

e) **Combine FOIR with behavioural analysis, not in isolation:** FOIR within or slightly above policy limits may still be unsafe if behavioural red flags exist; conversely, marginal FOIR breaches may be manageable where behaviour is impeccable and buffers are strong.

f) **Use calibrated decisions instead of binary thinking:** Advanced credit judgment often lies in structured partial approvals reducing quantum, tightening conditions, increasing pricing, and strengthening monitoring rather than mechanically choosing between full sanction and outright rejection.

Checklist: CIBIL Report Analysis

1. Confirm the report is freshly generated and never rely on an old report forwarded by the borrower or any agent.
2. Cross-check the Consumer or Entity Information block against KYC for spelling, DOB, and name sequence mismatches to avoid a wrong or merged file.
3. Treat any PAN mismatch as a hard stop and escalate for correction or bureau dispute before proceeding.
4. Record the report Control Number and generation timestamp in the appraisal notes for audit trail and future referencing.
5. If the score shows -1, 0, or NA, treat it as "untested risk" and lean more on bank statements, income proof, and field verification.
6. Verify that at least one loan account has been updated in the recent reporting window so the score reflects current behaviour, not stale history.
7. Use the score range only as an entry filter and make the decision only after reading accounts, remarks, and repayment patterns.
8. Read the DPD grid month-by-month and quantify repeated 30+ day delays instead of ignoring them as "minor".
9. Flag any SMA0, SMA1, SMA2, SUB, DBT, or LSS history as past stress even if the account is currently Standard.
10. Treat "Closed by Settlement" and "Written Off" remarks as major credit negatives regardless of the loan size.
11. Identify any restructuring history (including relief-period restructures) because a clean score can still hide grey stress.
12. Scrutinize OD or CC and credit card utilization, and treat sustained high utilization as a liquidity stress indicator.
13. Flag any over-limit or overdrawn utilization as a behavioural warning that the borrower operates without buffers.
14. Check for a shift from secured borrowing to unsecured borrowing because it often signals desperation for quick liquidity.

15. Analyse enquiries for clustering in short periods because enquiry spikes reveal loan shopping and credit hunger.
16. If large-ticket enquiries exist without corresponding active accounts, suspect rejections, unfulfilled borrowing attempts, or document-quality issues.
17. Watch for multiple small-ticket loans or frequent short-term borrowings because they often indicate rollover-style survival cash management.
18. Do not treat cheque bounce or EMI dishonour indicators as "minor" because even one can be an early signal of cash-flow breakage.
19. In Commercial CIBIL, treat CMR 7–10 as high-risk and require strong mitigants or avoid fresh exposure altogether.
20. Examine Relationship Details and Guarantor exposures, and insist on independent net worth of guarantors because cross-guarantees can be only paper comfort.
21. Cross-verify CIBIL with CRILC, deduplication checks, GST, and MCA data to detect hidden stress across lenders, disguised entities, and inflated turnover claims.

•••

CASE STUDY 4

THE BANK GUARANTEE TRAP: ONEROUS CLAUSES, OPEN-ENDED LIABILITY AND THE SILENT EROSION OF SURETY RIGHTS

Lessons for Sanctioning, Structuring, and Securing Large Bank Guarantee Limits

1. Introduction

This case examines the complex credit-risk issues faced by a bank while evaluating Bank Guarantee (BG) requests from a mid-sized EPC (Engineering, Procurement, and Construction) contractor engaged in national highway construction. While BGs appear to be non-fund based, they carry substantial contingent liabilities and can convert into immediate fund-based exposure if invoked.

The case highlights weaknesses in appraisal, contractual understanding, borrower capability assessment, and sanction conditions.

2. Borrower / Business Background

M/s. Highway InfraTech Pvt. Ltd. (HIPL), based in Ahmedabad, is a 12-year-old EPC contractor specializing in highways, bridges, and toll plaza construction.

Past performance:

- Completed 22 projects over 12 years.
- Average annual turnover: ₹320 crore.
- Current net worth: ₹72 crore.
- No history of BG invocation.
- Existing limits with the bank: Cash Credit: ₹45 crore, Term Loan (Machinery): ₹18 crore, BG limit: ₹40 crore.
- Collateral: Two commercial properties (valuation ₹70 crore).

HIPL applied to the bank for a significant enhancement of BG limits for a new NHAI contract.

3. Loan / Facility Requirement

HIPL has won a major NHAI contract:

Project: Six-lane upgrade of 42 km highway segment.

Contract Value: ₹600 crore.

Completion Period: 30 months.

Defect Liability Period: 12 months.

BG Requirements:

- Performance BG: ₹30 crore.
- Mobilisation Advance BG: ₹20 crore.
- Retention Money BG: ₹10 crore.
- Total Requested BG: ₹60 crore.

The borrower requested the BGs to be issued in favour of "National Highways Infrastructure Authority (NHIA)"- a PSU/government beneficiary.

4. Developments

During credit appraisal, several developments emerged:

a) **Aggressive BG Tenor Request:** HIPL requested that the Performance BG be issued for 4 years (30 months contract + 12 months defect liability + 6 months buffer). This exceeded the bank's usual comfort for non-AAA corporates (normally up to 3 years).

b) **Large Single BG Size:** The borrower intended to issue a single ₹30 crore BG, whereas its past largest BG was only ₹12 crore. This created capability mismatch risk.

c) **Third-Party Performance Risk:** HIPL intended to subcontract 55% of the project to minor contractors but wanted the bank to issue BG for full ₹30 crore, exposing the bank to third-party failure.

d) **Request for Interchangeability:** HIPL wanted free interchangeability between Performance BG and Financial BG (mobilisation BG), which represented materially different risk profiles.

e) **Onerous Clause Pressure from NHIA:** The beneficiary provided a BG text with:

- Auto-renewal clause.
- Invocation permitted on downgrade of the bank's credit rating.
- Validity: until NHIA issues discharge certificate (no fixed expiry).

  These were contractually dangerous for the bank.

f) **Collateral Tightness:** Existing collateral of ₹70 crore was already supporting all limits, including working capital. No fresh collateral was offered against the enhanced BG exposure.

5. Problem Statement

The bank's Credit Committee needed to decide:

a) Can a substantial BG enhancement be approved without proportional enhancement in collateral/security?

b) Should the bank accept onerous BG clauses demanded by the government body?

c) Is the borrower's execution capability sufficient to justify a single large BG?

d) How should the bank mitigate third-party subcontractor risks?

f) Can BG types be given interchangeability given their materially different risk levels?

This created credit dilemma for the bank's credit team.

6. Detailed Analysis

a. Assessment of Borrower Capability

HIPL's historical project execution never exceeded: a) Project size above ₹250 crore. b) Single BG above ₹12 crore.

Sanctioning a single ₹30 crore BG would allow HIPL to undertake a contract beyond demonstrated capability. As per internal credit policy, BG size must correlate with contractor capacity. A single large BG concentrates risk. If invoked, bank must pay entire amount immediately, affecting liquidity. Diversified, smaller BGs limit systemic risk.

Therefore, the credit team recommended: Maximum single BG ≤ ₹15 crore, even if total sanctioned BG limit is higher.

b. Tenor Risk & RBI Guidance

As per prudent practice and RBI's broad guidance:

- Longer-tenure BGs carry higher performance and counterparty uncertainty.
- Bank's risk appetite for non-AAA corporates is generally up to 3 years.

HIPL's request for 4+ years was considered excessive. So, Credit team recommended: Performance BG tenor = 3 years maximum, with mid-term review.

c. Financial BG vs Performance BG Risk

- Financial BGs are inherently riskier than performance BGs.
- Mobilisation advance BG (₹20 crore) is a financial BG, as the bank may need to pay if borrower misuses funds.
- Allowing interchangeability would convert lower-risk BGs to higher-risk BGs without assessment.

Credit team recommended: No interchangeability permitted between performance and financial BGs.

d. Third-Party / Subcontractor Risk

HIPL wanted the bank to issue BG for the full project, even though major components would be subcontracted. As per best practice:

- BG must be issued proportionate to the borrower's own scope of work, not for third-party obligations.
- Issuing a full BG becomes a third-party guarantee, prohibited under policy.

Credit team recommended: BG issuance only for the borrower's own contract share (45%).

e. BG Text - Onerous Clauses

NHIA insisted on clauses that were:

- Auto-renewal.
- Validity tied to beneficiary's discharge letter.
- Invocation permitted on rating downgrade.

These are onerous clauses that the bank should not accept without higher margin and policy approval. They compromise the bank's rights under Indian Contract Act (Surety rights).

Credit team recommended: Reject onerous clauses; issue BG only in bank's standard format.

f. Lack of Fresh Collateral

Total BG exposure sought = ₹60 crore.

Existing collateral = ₹70 crore (already supporting working capital + term loans).

Without additional collateral, the bank's coverage ratio would fall unacceptably below policy norms. Credit recommended:

- Cash margin minimum 25% for performance BG.
- Cash margin minimum 35% for financial BG.
- Fresh collateral of ₹30 crore required.

g. Cash Flow Routing

Given the sizeable BG exposure, the bank mandated:

- Mandatory routing of all project payments through borrower's account.
- Escrow mechanism for monitoring cash flows.

7. Applicable Laws / Regulations

Indian Contract Act, 1872

- BG = Contract of Guarantee; bank = Surety.
- Surety rights (Section 140, 141) must not be waived through onerous clauses.
- No BG should be open-ended or auto-renewing.

RBI Guidance

- Long-tenure guarantees discouraged (>10 years usually prohibited).
- Banks must maintain strict exposure and security coverage for contingent liabilities.
- Onerous BGs require board-level approval and additional margin.

8. Final Outcome / Decision

Approval Granted With Significant Modifications

a) **Overall BG Limit Enhanced:** The bank approved enhancement of the total Bank Guarantee limit to ₹60 crore, but only after restructuring the exposure into safer, controlled sub-limits.

b) **Revised Tenor Restrictions:**

- Performance BG: Limited to 36 months (contract period + reasonable claim period).
- Mobilisation Advance / Financial BG: Restricted to 18 months, with no rollover permitted without full review.

c) **Controlled Single BG Exposure:** The request for a single ₹30 crore BG was rejected.

A maximum single BG cap of ₹15 crore was imposed to prevent concentration risk and ensure alignment with the contractor's demonstrated execution history.

d) **Fresh Collateral Requirement:**

Based on risk rating and size of contingent exposure, the bank mandated additional collateral of ₹30 crore, ensuring security coverage remains within prudent norms.

e) **Cash Margin Conditions:**

25% for Performance BGs; 35% for Financial BGs. These higher margins reflect the varying risk levels between performance and financial obligations.

f) **Routing & Monitoring Conditions:**

- Mandatory routing of all project cash flows into the borrower's operative account with the bank.
- Establishment of an escrow mechanism for enhanced monitoring.
- Quarterly submission of project progress reports.

g) **Wording & Documentation Controls:** BGs would be issued only in the bank's standard format. All onerous clauses (auto-renewal, open-ended validity, invocation on rating downgrade) were rejected.

h) **Restrictions on Third-Party Risk:** The bank approved BG coverage only for HIPL's own contract share and disallowed BGs supporting subcontractor-controlled portions.

i) **Interchangeability Denied:** No interchangeability permitted between performance BG and financial BG due to differing risk profiles.

9. Key Lessons for Credit Professionals

a) BG size must correlate with demonstrated contractor capability; never sanction large single BGs without historic proof.

b) Financial BGs carry much higher invocation risk and require higher margins, stricter conditions, and shorter tenors.

c) Never allow BG issuance for third-party or subcontractor obligations. This becomes an unauthorized third-party guarantee.

d) Onerous clauses fundamentally compromise the bank's legal rights; always insist on standard BG wording unless fully secured.

e) Cash flow routing and collateral enhancement are essential to protect the bank when BG exposure becomes disproportionate to borrower strength.

Bank Guarantee Checklist for Credit Managers

1. Always verify that the BG tenor includes both the contract period and the claim period, ensuring total validity matches beneficiary requirements.
2. Clearly record BG commission and cash margin percentages in the sanction as per bank policy and risk grading.
3. Specify the exact type of BG (Performance / Financial / Counter BG) and document any permitted interchangeability in explicit numerical terms.
4. Confirm that the beneficiary name and category (Government/PSU/Corporate) are properly recorded and approved.
5. Ensure a cap on maximum single BG size based on borrower's historical project capability and execution profile.
6. Mandate routing of all project cash flows through the borrower's account with the bank for continuous monitoring.
7. Reject third-party BG exposure by issuing guarantees only for the borrower's proportionate contract share.

8. Prohibit issuance of BGs on behalf of group companies, subsidiaries, or associates unless specifically sanctioned.
9. Disallow BGs issued to support another bank's lending unless permitted under explicit policy with full appraisal.
10. Accept only standard BG wording and refuse any onerous clauses such as auto-renewals, open-ended validity, rating-based invocation, or waiver of surety rights.
11. Ensure collateral and margin adequacy aligns with enhanced contingent liability exposure.
12. Verify that subcontracting arrangements do not shift performance risk to the bank in cases where borrower outsources major work.
13. Assess the track record of past BG invocations, expiry compliance, and any history of delayed extensions.
14. Confirm that invocation notice requirements, including mode and branch address, align with bank's legal protections.
15. Validate that BGs have fixed, unambiguous expiry dates and no language that allows beneficiary discretion for validity extension.
16. Ensure counter BG structures are used only when transfer of collateral/ security between banks is fully secured and approved.
17. Evaluate the borrower's operational readiness, machinery capacity, manpower strength, and cash flow adequacy, to avoid over-commitment under high-value BGs.

18 Always cross-check whether the borrower has the technical and managerial depth to execute multiple BG-backed contracts simultaneously, preventing operational over-extension that leads to invocation.

•••

CASE STUDY 5

STREEDHAN, BULLET REPAYMENT AND THE HIDDEN EVERGREENING RISK BEHIND A KOZHIKODE IT BORROWER'S ₹5 LAKH GOLD LOAN

1. Introduction & Context

Kerala District Bank's Kozhikode Branch has a fast growing retail gold loan portfolio. For years, branch teams treated gold loans as fully secured and low risk, relying mostly on collateral weight and purity. With the RBI's current harmonised Directions on Lending Against Gold and Silver Collateral, that comfort has changed. Lenders must now factor cash flows, tiered Loan to Value caps, bullet repayment risks and ownership clarity.

2. Borrower Background

Mr. Arjun Nambiar, aged 31, works as a software engineer with Malabar Digital Systems Pvt Ltd, an IT company operating from the Kozhikode IT park. His income is stable but skewed, with a fixed monthly salary and a chunky annual bonus that depends on project performance and global budgets. EMI outgo on a home loan, school fees and car loan already absorb a significant portion of his fixed pay.

Arjun's wife, Meera Nambiar, is a homemaker. Most of the family's gold is her bridal jewellery and gifts received from her parents and in laws. In their minds this is typical "streedhan" that emotionally belongs to Meera, even though it physically lies in a bank locker. When Arjun needs quick cash for medical expenses and to close some high cost personal debt, he chooses a gold loan at Kozhikode Branch, using Meera's ornaments as collateral.

3. Type of Facility Requested

Arjun applies for a ₹5,00,000 consumption gold loan at Kerala District Bank, Kozhikode Branch. The product offered is:

- Loan against pledge of household gold jewellery.

- Tenor 12 months.
- Bullet repayment structure where both principal and interest fall due at maturity.
- Pricing linked to the bank's retail gold loan card rate.

Under the current RBI Directions, such a loan is a consumption loan against eligible gold collateral and must respect tiered LTV caps. For total consumption loans per borrower above ₹2.5 lakh and up to ₹5 lakh, the maximum LTV is 80 percent. For bullet loans, LTV must be computed on the total amount payable at maturity, not just the principal.

Further, once loans against eligible collateral to a borrower exceed ₹2.5 lakh, the lender is required to carry out a detailed credit assessment and repayment capacity evaluation, rather than treating it as collateral only lending.

4. Major Developments

At origination, the file looks straightforward. Meera accompanies Arjun to the branch and hands over her jewellery. The bank's empanelled assayer verifies purity and weight inside the branch, in their presence, and issues an assay certificate(lab test of purity) detailing gross weight, net gold weight after deductions for stones and fastenings, purity and value. A copy is given to the borrower, a copy stays in the loan file.

Using the lower of the preceding 30 day average gold price and the previous day's price from IBJA or a SEBI regulated exchange, the branch calculates intrinsic value and sanctions ₹5 lakh at within 80 percent LTV on this value. The aggregate pledged weight is within the new 1 kilogram per borrower cap for gold ornaments. The loan agreement describes item wise collateral, value, auction conditions and timelines for release on repayment.

Procedurally, most boxes seem ticked. The ornaments are sealed in the branch under camera, in the presence of the assayer, borrower, Meera and the officer, and placed in the vault. Gold Ornament Register and Gold Bag Register entries are made, mapping the loan account to a unique sealed packet number, in line with good practice explained in the internal gold loan verification master circular of the bank.

Two developments change the risk profile. First, three months later Arjun's salary credits become irregular because his employer delays variable pay and there are rumours of downsizing. Second, he asks for a top up and hints that if the bank cannot extend more, he may seek a rollover at maturity. Under the current Directions, renewals or top ups on gold loans are allowed only if the account is standard, only within permissible LTV and, in case of bullet loans, only after payment of accrued interest.

Meera's body language also changes. She appears uncomfortable that her streedhan is locked for a full year and quietly asks the officer what happens if Arjun changes jobs or delays repayment. For a young credit professional, these human cues become as important as ratios.

5. Problem Statement

a) The pledged jewellery is Meera's streedhan and there is a visible change in her comfort level after sanction, raising a real possibility of future ownership or consent disputes if recovery or auction is triggered.

b) The ₹5 lakh bullet loan sits at the upper end of the 2.5 to 5 lakh slab, and with interest added at maturity, the true LTV on the total payable can easily creep close to the 80 percent cap if gold prices soften.

c) Arjun's repayment plan relies heavily on an uncertain annual bonus, while his fixed salary is already strained by existing EMIs, increasing the risk that the bullet obligation may not be met on time even though collateral is strong.

d) The borrower is already seeking a top up within the first quarter of tenor, which, combined with salary irregularity, is an early warning signal that this gold loan may slip from clean liquidity support into hidden stress management and evergreening pressure.

6. Detailed Analysis

6.1 Bullet structure, LTV and cash flows

Under the current Directions, bullet repayment for consumption gold loans is permitted but the tenor is capped at 12 months, and lenders must compute LTV using the total amount payable at maturity. For a ₹5 lakh loan at a typical retail gold loan rate, the maturity amount could be materially higher once interest is included. If gold prices fall or remain flat, the collateral cushion shrinks.

For Kerala District Bank, Kozhikode, this means that even if the origination LTV is within 80 percent, ongoing LTV monitoring is mandatory through the tenor. Any top up cannot be allowed merely because "gold value has gone up" unless updated valuation, maturity amount and revised LTV are documented.

6.2 Ownership, streedhan and enforceability

The Directions clearly state that lenders must not extend loans where collateral ownership is doubtful and must obtain a declaration from the borrower that they are the rightful owner of the collateral. In Indian households, streedhan jewellery is often legally and emotionally treated as the woman's property. The bank did take Meera's KYC and signature at sanction, but the consent format is generic. If the relationship sours or if there is any dispute during auction, a weak streedhan consent can quickly become a litigation point.

Internal gold verification guidance already emphasised that where ladies' ornaments and streedhan are pledged, explicit consent of the lady is critical to create an enforceable charge. Under the current framework, such ownership clarity is also a conduct and AML expectation.

6.3 Collateral management and customer protection

The current Directions demand that gold handling must be done only in branches, only by employees, and stored only in branches with safe vaults, with periodic surprise verification and internal audit. The Kozhikode branch has complied structurally, but documentation must be robust enough for any future complaint.

The assay certificate, with images and deductions, is now a key defence document, not a formality. The loan agreement must also capture timelines for release and auction procedure, including the rule that pledged collateral must be returned within a maximum of seven working days after full repayment, failing which the lender may have to compensate the borrower at ₹5,000 per day of delay.

These customer protection obligations give Meera strong rights. If the bank mishandles auction or delays release of her jewellery after closure, compensation and reputational impact will follow.

6.4 Renewal, top up and evergreening risk

The current Directions permit renewal and top up only where the loan is standard, LTV is within permitted band and, for bullet loans, only after interest is paid. They also require that such renewals be clearly identifiable in the core banking system to prevent disguised evergreening.

Arjun is seeking a top up early, while salary inflows are already irregular. If the branch simply extends more money against the same packet, or "closes" the old bullet with a fresh bullet without genuine interest servicing, it would violate these conditions and mask stress. For a new underwriter, this is the real test: saying no to an apparently safe, fully secured top up when the behaviour pattern is wrong.

7. Outcome / Final Decision

The bank's credit team decides not to sanction any top up and not to allow a like for like bullet renewal at maturity. Instead, they rework the facility within the existing ₹5 lakh exposure.

The loan is converted from a pure bullet structure into a hybrid repayment schedule for the remaining tenor, with monthly interest servicing and two structured principal instalments, to reduce the maturity bulge and improve behaviour visibility. A fresh credit assessment is done, including salary slips, bank statements and updated employer confirmation, in line with the requirement for detailed assessment above ₹2.5 lakh.

As conditions precedent, Meera signs a strengthened streedhan consent and ownership declaration that specifically lists each ornament as per the assay certificate. The bank re values the gold using the latest 30 day price rule, confirms that even on the higher maturity amount the LTV stays within 80 percent, and records this in the file.

As conditions subsequent, the branch agrees to monitor LTV on a quarterly basis and to flag this account in internal gold loan MIS as "behaviour watch" because of the early top up request and salary volatility. Any further request for restructuring or renewal will go to Regional/Zonal Office for approval, not just the branch manager.

8. Key Learnings for Credit Professionals

a) Insist on explicit streedhan ownership and consent documentation whenever a spouse's jewellery is pledged, because collateral control without clear title is an illusion.

b) Treat bullet gold loans above ₹2.5 lakh as full credit files that need cash flow assessment and ongoing LTV monitoring, not as mere gram based transactions.

c) Use the assay certificate, image record and loan agreement as litigation grade documents by ensuring they capture valuation basis, auction rules and release timelines in line with RBI Directions.

d) Refuse early top ups or rollovers in gold loans when behaviour and income signals are weak, even if the packet is heavy, because evergreening under a "fully secured" label is still evergreening.

Gold Loans Checklist for Credit Professionals

1) Verify borrower KYC first, and if the gold loan is being given to an existing savings account customer, confirm that the savings account KYC is fully compliant.

2) Check product-wise maximum permissible limits strictly (including agriculture gold loans where policy may cap at ₹3 lakh and require valid 7/12 land extract), and flag any sanction above policy as an adverse deviation.

3) Confirm margin is as per policy (often 20 - 30%) and ensure the bank's internal lending rate for gold is applied rather than pure market rate while computing eligible loan amount.

4) Ensure the gold loan application is complete and core documents like Demand Promissory Note, Promissory Note and Letter of Continuity are executed in the prescribed formats.

5) Validate that stamp duty and pledge-related charges (where applicable under the bank's documentation practice) are properly paid and recorded, especially for running facilities like Gold CC/OD where renewals are frequently missed.

6) Where pledged ornaments are women's ornaments or streedhan items (mangalsutra, bridal jewellery), obtain explicit consent of the lady owner to avoid enforceability disputes later.

7) Conduct valuation and sealing inside the branch in the presence of the borrower, valuer and bank officials, with ornaments packed first in a plastic bag and then a cloth bag containing an item list, and avoid any process where the borrower carries gold outside to the valuer.
8) At release, verify the seal matches original sealing, open only in the presence of required parties, and prepare a proper panchnama to prevent later allegations of replacement or tampering.
9) Maintain Gold Ornament Register and Gold Bag Register with ornament-wise detail and reconcile outstanding gold loan accounts to physical gold bags in custody, and ensure approved valuer credentials, security deposit, bond validity and valuer rotation are current.
10) During audit or surprise checks, never open any gold bag independently, and if sample verification is required, do it with borrower, valuer and bank officer present, using the same valuation method, with a second valuer if needed.
11) Value collateral using RBI's reference-price method (lower of 30-day average closing or previous day closing from IBJA or SEBI-regulated exchange), and consider only intrinsic metal value excluding stones or gems.
12) Apply RBI's tiered LTV caps for consumption loans (≤₹2.5 lakh: 85%, >₹2.5 - ₹5 lakh: 80%, >₹5 lakh: 75%) and maintain the prescribed LTV on an ongoing basis through the tenor(* or use as per your bank's guidelines).
13) For bullet repayment loans, compute "loan amount" for LTV as the total amount payable at maturity, not merely the principal outstanding.
14) Issue the RBI-required assay certificate or e-certificate in duplicate (purity, gross and net weight, deductions, defects, image, value), keep one in file and hand one to the borrower under acknowledgement, and release pledged collateral within seven working days of full repayment or compensate ₹5,000 per day for lender-attributable delay.
15) Institutionalise a "gold loan discipline pack" by forcing maker-checker vault access with daily bag-count sign-off, CIF-level monitoring for multiple/frequent gold loans to spot structuring and collusion early, and a stress-tested LTV buffer policy that assumes interest accrual plus a conservative gold-price fall before approving renewals or top-ups.

•••

CASE STUDY 6

WHEN CHARGES COLLIDE: FIRST CHARGE, PARI PASSU CHARGE & SECOND CHARGE IN A MULTI-LENDER BATTLE

How Overlapping Security Structures can trap even a performing borrower into lender conflict

1. Introduction

This case explores a credit scenario involving a mid-sized engineering manufacturing unit whose aggressive multi-banking expansion created overlapping charge structures, disputed priorities, and legal vulnerabilities during stress. It demonstrates how improper charge management can convert an otherwise solvent business into a high-risk exposure for lenders, highlighting the need for credit officers to deeply understand first charge, pari passu rights, and subordinate security implications.

2. Borrower Background

M/s TechForge Precision Components Pvt. Ltd., based in Gujarat, manufactures precision-engineered components used in industrial machinery. Over 12 years, the company scaled to a turnover of ₹82 crore with moderate profitability. Management is experienced but aggressive in expansion, frequently refinancing and adding banking partners.

The company operates from a large industrial unit comprising land, building, CNC machinery, and robotic fabrication lines. These fixed assets form the backbone of the company's banking security structure.

3. Type of Loan / Facility Details

TechForge avails facilities from three lenders:

a) **Bank Orion**

- ₹18 crore Term Loan
- ₹10 crore Cash Credit
- Exclusive First Charge on land, building, and all existing machinery.

b) Nova Industrial Bank

- ₹16 crore Cash Credit (multiple banking)
- First charge on current assets,
- Second Charge on fixed assets.

c) Axis Mercantile Finance Ltd. (NBFC)

- ₹12 crore Machinery Loan
- Requested pari passu charge on some machinery;
- Bank Orion permitted only a restricted pari passu on new machinery purchased from NBFC's finance but retained first charge on old assets.

The borrower kept all three lenders satisfied initially, but the complex layering of charges created a legal and operational minefield.

Lets first discuss what all these charges means:

a) First Charge (Exclusive / Primary Charge)

A First Charge means the lender has the highest and exclusive right over a specific asset.

If the borrower defaults, this lender gets paid first from the sale proceeds of that asset before any other lender. It offers the strongest security comfort.

b) Pari Passu Charge (Equal Ranking Charge)

A Pari Passu Charge means two or more lenders share the same security on equal footing.

During enforcement, the sale proceeds of the asset are shared proportionately among all pari passu lenders, normally in the ratio of their outstanding dues. No lender has superior rights over the others.

c) Second Charge (Subordinate Charge)

A Second Charge gives the lender a subordinate right over the asset.

This lender gets paid only after the first charge holder's entire dues are cleared. Recovery depends fully on whether any surplus remains after satisfying the first charge holder.

4. Scenario & Developments

TechForge secured a large order from an overseas client requiring volume expansion. Management hurriedly purchased machinery using NBFC funding before receiving formal NOCs from existing banks. Simultaneously, cash flow pressures led to delays in servicing Bank Orion's term loan.

As repayment delays stretched beyond 60 days, Bank Orion initiated internal SMA tracking. Meanwhile, Nova Bank observed stock shortages and a sharp drop in receivable quality. To bridge working capital gaps, the promoter diverted receivables to an unsecured fintech lender without informing the existing charge holders, thereby breaching the agreed security terms and conditions governing the facility.

Trouble escalated when the NBFC claimed pari passu rights over all machinery, pointing to an ambiguous clause in its loan agreement. Bank Orion strongly disputed this, insisting that its exclusive first charge remained intact.

The stage was now set for a multi-lender conflict.

5. Problem Statement

a) Ambiguous charge creation on machinery, causing conflict between Bank Orion's exclusive first charge and the NBFC's claimed pari passu rights.

b) Creation of undisclosed encumbrances on mortgaged security, where the borrower raised a facility from a fintech lender and created fresh charges on the same collateral without informing the existing lenders or obtaining their mandatory NOC.

c) Inadequate ROC/CERSAI updates, resulting in legal ambiguity on actual ranking and nature of charges.

d) Asset value erosion risk, as fixed assets significantly depreciated while combined debt obligations increased.

e) Operational stress and liquidity crunch due to delayed receivables and diversion of working capital, increasing probability of account classification as NPA.

6. Detailed Analysis & Discussion

TechForge's situation reflects a classic credit pitfall: excessive leveraging of the same security across multiple lenders without disciplined inter-creditor coordination. The manufacturing unit's fixed assets were the foundation of Bank Orion's lending comfort. Its first charge was clear in the mortgage and hypothecation deeds.

However, when the NBFC financed new machinery, it drafted a facility agreement indicating "pari passu charge over the borrower's machinery assets." This clause, though intended only for the newly purchased machines, did not explicitly restrict its scope. The borrower exploited this ambiguity to obtain faster disbursement.

Bank Orion issued a limited NOC but delayed updating CERSAI. The NBFC immediately registered a broad charge covering entire machinery block, creating a documentary conflict. Nova Bank, which held second charge on fixed assets, raised objections as its priority was also compromised. This inconsistency in registrations became the root of later legal disputes.

Parallelly, the borrower's stress over a large export order created pressure on working capital. Receivables stretched beyond 120 days, stock turnover slowed, and current asset coverage deteriorated. Nova Bank's monthly stock inspections showed declining raw material levels despite rising drawing power utilisation.

To avoid drawing power reduction, the borrower sold finished goods at a discount and diverted the proceeds to an unsecured fintech lender, an act that violated the negative lien clause and weakened existing primary security.

During SMA-2 classification, all lenders sought clarity on recoverability. Bank Orion, with first charge, could enforce SARFAESI and direct sale of land, building, and existing machinery. Nova Bank, as second charge holder, would only receive surplus after Orion's full recovery, highly unlikely given low forced-sale value. The NBFC's pari passu claim hinged on whether its charge was legally perfected and whether Bank Orion's NOC restricted rights only to new machinery.

Legal counsel warned that if the dispute reached IBC, the resolution professional might treat both lenders as pari passu depending on documents, leaving Orion exposed to a larger haircut. Ultimately, inconsistent documentation, poor inter-lender coordination, and borrower opportunism created a fragile security structure.

7. Outcome / Final Decision

After prolonged negotiation, all lenders agreed to a structured resolution:

a) Bank Orion's first charge was reaffirmed on land, building, and entire old machinery block.

b) NBFC's pari passu right was restricted strictly to new machinery financed by it, after a corrected CERSAI filing.

c) Nova Bank continued as second charge holder, with reinstated priority following corrected filings.

d) Borrower executed a revised Inter-Creditor Understanding (ICU) defining enforcement priorities.

e) Promoter infused ₹3 crore as additional margin to stabilize operations.

f) A monitored escrow was created to prevent receivable diversion.

g) Banks agreed to a controlled restructuring under RBI guidelines, extending TL tenor by two years.

The account was downgraded but avoided NPA classification due to timely restructuring and promoter support.

8. Key Lessons for Credit Professionals

a) Never rely solely on the sanction letter, charge ranking must match ROC and CERSAI filings for legal perfection.

b) In multi-lender cases, insist on precise, unambiguous language defining whether charge is exclusive, pari passu, or second charge.

c) Document every NOC carefully; a loosely drafted clause can distort priority and expose the bank to severe recovery risks.

d) Second charge recovery is inherently uncertain. Always assess realisable value after first charge holder recovery.

e) Regular monitoring of ROC/CERSAI ensures early detection of undisclosed charges created with fintechs or NBFCs.

f) Always evaluate security in combined terms, not standalone, when pari passu or subordinate lenders exist.

First vs. Pari Passu vs. Second Charge

Aspect	First Charge	Pari Passu Charge	Second Charge
Priority on Enforcement	Highest among secured lenders on that asset	Equal priority with other pari passu lenders	After first charge dues are recovered
Comfort Level	Highest (subject to value)	Medium – depends on total shared exposure	Relatively low, depends on surplus
Typical Usage	Term loans, LAP, exclusive security	Consortium working capital, shared collateral	Additional WC / top-up on same security
Key Requirement	Clear, exclusive documentation & registration	Strong inter-creditor agreement, proper sharing	Clarity on subordination, realistic valuation
Pricing / Margin	Can be lower (other factors equal)	Moderate	Usually higher pricing / stronger conditions

•••

CASE STUDY 7

STABLE SALARY, SLIPPING CONTROLS: THE ₹11 LAKH CAR LOAN TO A PSU OFFICER AT JAISALMER

1. Introduction

Marudhara Bank's Jaisalmer branch had a clear business focus: grow retail assets in a border district with strong salaried clientele from the armed forces, paramilitary, and public sector undertakings (PSUs). Vehicle loans were the star product - quick to sell, easy to explain, backed by a tangible asset.

For newly joined credit officers, the message was simple: *"Government salary hai, gaadi loan safe hai." ("Government salary is there so Vehicle loan is safe")*

This case shows how that comfort nearly turned into complacency when a straightforward ₹11 lakh car loan to a disciplined PSU officer posted at Jaisalmer started showing cracks - not because the borrower was dishonest, but because basic vehicle-loan discipline was diluted at multiple stages.

2. Borrower Background

The borrower, Mr. Vikram Shekhawat, was working as an Officer in a Public Sector Undertaking (PSU) and posted at Jaisalmer.

- Age: 32 years.

- Service: 9 years of continuous service in the PSU.

- Salary: Credited to his salary account with Marudhara Bank, Jaisalmer.

- Family: Married, one child, living in rented accommodation.

Vikram wanted to purchase a new compact SUV to commute between his PSU office, nearby project sites, and his family's home in town. He positioned the loan as a long-term family asset and relied heavily on his "secure government-linked income" as his selling point.

3. Type of Loan / Facility Details

Facility: Car Loan – New Vehicle.

Bank: Marudhara Bank, Jaisalmer Branch.

Vehicle: New compact SUV (diesel).

On-road cost (invoice + RTO + first-year insurance): Approx. ₹13.5 lakh.

Sanctioned loan amount: ₹11 lakh.

Margin as per policy: 20% of eligible cost.

Tenor: 84 months.

Repayment: EMI through NACH from salary account.

Security: Hypothecation of vehicle in favour of Marudhara Bank.

For bank, the proposal looked ideal: stable PSU salary, visible asset, and a competitive product in a branch that understood salaried government and PSU customers well.

4. Major Developments

At the appraisal stage, the young credit officer derived Vikram's monthly net salary after deductions and checked that the proposed EMI, along with existing obligations, broadly fit within the bank's permitted Fixed Obligation to Income Ratio (FOIR). CIBIL showed an existing small personal loan with good repayment track record.

The loan was sanctioned quickly. The branch collected margin in Vikram's savings account and prepared to disburse. Here, operational convenience overtook discipline. Instead of making a direct payment to the car dealer, the branch, pressed by month-end targets and the borrower's request to "first credit my account and I will swipe at the showroom," routed the entire ₹11 lakh into Vikram's savings account.

The vehicle was actually purchased, but a few procedural corners were cut:

- Margin payment trail was not fully evidenced from bank records.
- RC book took longer than expected to be submitted.
- One year later, insurance renewal slipped through the cracks.

After about 18 months, EMIs began bouncing intermittently when Vikram's allowances and certain variable components reduced due to internal policy changes and some additional deductions. The account slipped into SMA status, prompting a detailed file review by the branch credit head.

5. Problem Statement

a) FOIR and income capacity were assessed, but other deductions and obligations were not documented comprehensively, making repayment comfort more optimistic than reality.

b) Disbursement of the loan amount was routed through the borrower's savings account instead of direct dealer payment, weakening end-use control.

c) Complete evidence of margin contribution from the borrower to the dealer through banking channels was not maintained.

d) RC book with proper hypothecation in favour of Marudhara Bank was not obtained within a reasonable time, and follow-up was not documented rigorously.

e) Insurance renewal was not tracked systematically, and the vehicle remained uninsured for a period while EMIs had already started becoming irregular.

6. Detailed Analysis

6.1 Stage 1 - Credit Appraisal

At first glance, Vikram's income profile appeared strong. His PSU officer grade, fixed salary, and government-linked job stability gave comfort. The officer checked salary slips and account credits, derived a monthly net take-home and confirmed that, including the proposed EMI and a small existing loan, obligations were roughly within the branch's 50 - 60% take-home threshold.

However, the appraisal had two weak points:

i) Other bank relationships and off-statement deductions (such as society installments and a small consumer loan) were not fully captured despite hints in the CIBIL report.

ii) The appraisal note stated "PSU job - stable customer," but did not clearly document a detailed working of net disposable income and sensitivity to future changes in allowances and deductions.

Technically, the loan was within policy, but the file did not tell a clear, defensible story of "how much EMI can he really afford comfortably."

6.2 Stage 2 - Sanction & Disbursement

Sanction terms - loan amount, tenor, ROI, margin - were aligned with policy. Where discipline slipped was disbursement:

i) The correct approach, as per bank norms, was to ensure that borrower margin plus loan proceeds together went directly to the dealer's account, backed by receipts and invoice.

ii) Instead, the branch credited the full ₹11 lakh to Vikram's savings account and relied on him to pay the dealer. This created classic end-use risk: once funds touch the borrower's account, diversion is possible and the defence that "we financed the car" weakens.

In this case, Vikram did buy the car, but from a control perspective, the branch could not demonstrate a clean, straight-through payment trail. Additionally, the final invoice reflected a slightly higher variant cost, and margin sufficiency was not re-checked against the upgraded on-road price.

6.3 Stage 3 – Documentation

Documentation was mostly complete at execution: loan agreement, hypothecation deed, NACH mandate, and first-year insurance policy were all in place. The gaps emerged in post-disbursement follow-through:

RC book: The branch expected the RC within 3 - 4 months. It did not arrive, and follow-up remained verbal. There was no systematic follow-up, no escalation, and no written reminders. When the account turned SMA, the credit head found that RC with hypothecation endorsement was still not on file.

Insurance: The first-year policy naming the bank as hypothecatee was on record, but no renewal control was set. After the first year, the policy lapsed for some time before the branch noticed it during SMA review.

Thus, while the security existed physically, the legal and documentary grip on it was weaker than what a vehicle loan demands.

6.4 Stage 4 - Review, Monitoring & Supervision

The first EMI bounce was treated as a minor issue and re-presentation was done. As bounces repeated, the account slipped into the SMA bucket. Only then did the branch undertake a structured review:

- They met Vikram, understood that changed salary components and extra deductions had squeezed his take-home income.
- They inspected the vehicle, confirmed its existence and usage, and finally obtained the RC, ensuring hypothecation in favour of Marudhara Bank was correctly endorsed.
- They insisted on immediate insurance renewal with the bank's interest noted in the policy.
- A stricter monitoring plan was agreed: standing instructions from salary, early alerts for any future bounce, and clear communication that, if irregularity continued, repossession as per bank policy would follow.

The account eventually regularised as Vikram adjusted his other commitments and received certain arrears and reimbursements from his PSU employer. But the branch clearly saw how close a "safe salaried car loan" had come to slipping towards NPA due to soft controls.

7. Outcome / Final Decision

The Jaisalmer branch did not restructure the loan but took firm corrective steps:

- It regularised documentation by obtaining the RC with hypothecation and updated insurance.
- It documented a detailed income and obligation assessment, correcting the weak appraisal narrative.
- It placed the account under closer monitoring, with clear early-warning flags and escalation thresholds.

Vikram, recognising the seriousness and wanting to protect both his credit history and his vehicle, prioritised clearing overdue EMIs. Within a few months, the loan returned to regular status. The branch, however, treated the episode as a training case for new credit staff on how even a "comfortable" PSU profile can hide process risk if basic vehicle loan disciplines are ignored.

8. Key Lessons for Credit Professionals

a) Do not be blinded by "secure salary" - always document a clear, numbers-backed FOIR and repayment analysis.

b) Insist on direct dealer payments with full evidence of borrower margin; avoid routing large disbursements via the borrower's account.

c) Treat RC hypothecation and insurance renewal as non-negotiable controls, not mere paperwork.

d) Use SMA movement as an early warning to re-check both documentation and borrower cash flows, not just to chase cheques.

e) Convert such near-miss cases into internal learning tools so that new officers embed vehicle-loan discipline from day one.

Vehicle Loans Checklist for Credit Professionals

1) Ensure the borrower's total EMI obligations, including the proposed vehicle loan, remain within the bank's FOIR limit after verifying salary slips, ITRs, and existing loan statements.

2) Cross-check the credit bureau report for write-offs, settlements, recent delinquencies, and enquiry spikes before concluding that the borrower is "standard."

3) Confirm that the vehicle quotation or proforma invoice is genuine, model-specific, and issued by an acceptable dealer with all cost components clearly itemised.

4) Validate that the borrower's margin contribution has actually been paid to the dealer through banking channels and is evidenced by receipts or bank statements.

5) Insist that the entire loan amount is disbursed directly to the dealer (or as per approved exception policy) to minimise diversion and "paper vehicle" risk.

6) Check that all loan and hypothecation documents are duly executed, correctly stamped as per state law, and completed without blanks or unauthorised overwriting.

7) Verify the insurance policy for correct IDV(Insurance Declared Valuc), inclusion of own-damage and third-party cover, and proper noting of the bank's hypothecation clause, with renewal tracking diarised.

8) Obtain the Registration Certificate and ensure hypothecation in favour of the bank is endorsed, recorded, and where feasible cross-verified on VAHAN or the relevant RTO system.

9) Ensure post-disbursement inspection of the vehicle is conducted within the stipulated timeline, capturing chassis and engine numbers, location, and condition with supporting evidence.

10) For used vehicle loans, insist on an independent valuation, confirm the odometer reading and year of manufacture, and check that LTV and tenor comply with policy for vehicle age.

11) Review the NACH/ECS mandate for accuracy of account number, IFSC, EMI amount, and start date, and confirm that the registration status is successful in the bank's system.

12) Assess borrower stability by examining employment continuity, length of current residence, and main account conduct so that the facility remains cash-flow-backed, not merely asset-backed.

13) Set clear early-warning triggers such as first EMI bounce, repeated mandate re-presentations, or irregular part payments and ensure timely, documented follow-up and escalation.

14) Ensure the loan agreement clearly defines repossession and sale rights and that branch staff are trained on compliant seizure and auction processes to avoid legal disputes.

15) Periodically review the vehicle loan portfolio for concentration by dealer, geography, or sourcing channel and investigate dealers or DSAs with disproportionately high delinquency or repossession cases.

•••

CASE STUDY 8

THE PLEDGED STOCK MIRAGE: HOW ONE COMMODITY TRADER EXPLOITED WAREHOUSE RECEIPT FINANCE – AND HOW THE CREDIT TEAM RESPONDED

1. Introduction

Pledge Finance / Warehouse Receipt Finance is intended to be one of the safest working-capital products in banking. The logic is simple: the stock itself is the primary security. If the stock exists, is of acceptable quality, and lies in a controlled warehouse with the bank's lien, the bank's exposure should remain adequately protected.

But this assurance holds only when procedures are followed perfectly i.e. from warehouse verification to lien marking, insurance, periodic inspections, MTM margining, and prevention of double financing. This case examines how a mid-sized commodity trader attempted to exploit procedural gaps in a medium-risk warehouse. The bank's credit team detected multiple red flags, some subtle, some obvious and finally prevented a potential loss.

2. Borrower / Business Background

M/s Shivhari Commodities, a proprietorship firm based in Andhra Pradesh, is engaged in trading processed rice and paddy. The proprietor, Mr. Raghav Singh, has been banking with Suryodaya Bank Ltd. (SBL) for the past three years under a ₹3 crore CC limit based on stock and receivables. After a strong harvest season and rising off-season price expectations, Mr. Singh approached SBL for a separate Warehouse Receipt Finance (WRF) limit of ₹2 crore, claiming that he intended to store high-grade rice in a warehouse empanelled with the bank.

3. Type of Facility Requested

Facility: Pledge Finance / Warehouse Receipt Finance.

Tenor: 12 months (short-term WC).

Security: Warehouse Receipts with lien in favour of the bank.

Additional Collateral: None proposed (standard for pledge finance).

Margin: 30% promoter margin + 5% initial margin (as per bank policy).

Warehouse Proposed: "Prashant Agro Warehousing Pvt. Ltd." – a licensed private warehouse, not WDRA-registered.

4. Major Developments

When the borrower submitted his proposal for a separate pledge finance facility, the documentation initially appeared routine. He produced physical warehouse receipts showing substantial quantities of Grade-I rice stored in a licensed private warehouse. The declared market value suggested a strong off-season trading strategy, and the borrower pushed for quick disbursement, citing immediate business opportunities.

However, as the credit team proceeded with standard verification, certain inconsistencies emerged. The warehouse chosen was not among the bank's preferred high-control locations, and the receipts had been issued only a few days prior. Market intelligence and internal checks also indicated that the declared price of the commodity was significantly higher than prevailing rates for the same grade, raising doubts about valuation accuracy.

Further scrutiny of the borrower's existing CC stock statements revealed an unusual overlap between the stock declared under CC limits and the stock now being offered under pledge finance. This overlap hinted at a potential attempt to secure funding twice against the same commodity, prompting deeper investigation and on-ground verification.

5. Problem Statement

Five core concerns emerged:

i) The warehouse was licensed but not WDRA-registered, increasing both operational and collusion risk.

ii) The borrower had recently shifted from lower-value paddy to higher-value rice, raising suspicion of valuation manipulation.

iii) The receipts were physical and non-negotiable, requiring more stringent controls; the borrower insisted on "urgent disbursement".

iv) Market prices for the claimed rice grade did not match the values declared, pointing towards inflated valuation.

v) There were signs of attempted double financing: the same stock appeared partially reflected in the borrower's CC stock statements.

6. Detailed Analysis & Discussion

6.1 Warehouse Verification Findings

A joint visit by the branch and empanelled quality expert uncovered severe irregularities:

- Bags labelled as Grade I from outside were found to be mixed quality internally.
- Sampling revealed moisture levels above the acceptable threshold.
- Several stacks were covered with tarpaulin; dust marks indicated recent movement, not stable storage.
- Out of 1,200 MT shown in the receipt, only 870 MT was physically traceable during inspection.

As per norms, documents of title do not guarantee the contents of the package; hence physical inspection is mandatory.

6.2 Receipt Documentation Issues

- Receipts were issued only 3 days before loan application, contrary to the need for avoiding old or manipulated receipts.
- Endorsement to the bank was incomplete; the warehouseman had not yet acknowledged lien marking.

6.3 Insurance Red Flags

As per regulatory guidance, stocks must be insured for their full cost or market value, and the policy must be verified and recorded in branch books before disbursement. The borrower submitted only a photocopy of an insurance policy, and even that was deficient on two critical counts: it carried no warehouse location endorsement and no specific commodity description, both of which are essential for any valid claim. When the insurer was independently contacted, the policy number was confirmed valid, but the sum insured was only ₹40 lakh against stock valued at over ₹1 crore, a case of severe under-insurance.

6.4 Price Verification & Margin Concerns

Quality expert reports showed:

- Actual market rate of that rice variety: ₹72 - ₹76/kg.
- Borrower's declared value: ₹100/kg.

With promoter margin of 30% and additional 5% initial margin, the bank was effectively financing nearly 100% of the real market value which was completely unacceptable. As per mark-to-market norms:

Banks must raise margin calls when commodity prices fall beyond the initial margin buffer.

Here, the borrower had created artificial inflation in the "base price", distorting the risk profile.

6.5 Indications of Double Financing

During the DP review of the existing CC limit, the stock statement included: 850 MT rice (Grade unspecified) stored "offsite".

A cross-check revealed that the location mentioned corresponded to Prashant Agro Warehousing Pvt. Ltd., the same warehouse used for pledge finance.

As per norms: Stock financed under pledge cannot again generate DP under CC. It must be either excluded from stock or adjusted against the CC DP. The borrower was attempting to leverage the same stock for two separate limits.

7. Outcome / Final Decision

After consolidating all findings, the credit team concluded:

a) The warehouse was acceptable only under stringent controls, not under the relaxed model requested by the borrower.

b) Physical stock shortage (870 MT vs 1,200 MT) made disbursement unsafe.

c) Under-insurance and poor quality violated core pledge-finance principles.

d) Valuation inflation distorted margin adequacy.

e) Attempted double financing breached credit discipline and raised integrity concerns.

Accordingly, SBL rejected the WRF proposal and simultaneously:

- Issued an Early Warning Signal (EWS) in the borrower's CC account.
- Revised DP calculations to exclude suspect stock.
- Ordered a full stock audit of the CC limit.
- Directed the borrower to regularize stock insurance immediately.
- Updated internal warehouse empanelment guidelines for private warehouses.

The timely intervention prevented a potential loss estimated at ₹60–70 lakh in case of borrower default and distressed stock liquidation.

8. Key Learnings for Credit Professionals

a) Never rely on the warehouse receipt alone, always perform physical inspection, especially in private non-WDRA warehouses.

b) Strictly prevent double financing by adjusting pledged stock against CC DP calculations as per policy.

c) Always validate commodity quality, grade, insurance coverage, and actual market price before sanction or disbursement.

d) Treat rushed applications and inflated valuations as immediate red flags requiring intensified scrutiny.

Advanced Checklist for Pledge Finance

1. Ensure that goods are already stored in an approved warehouse and that a valid warehouse receipt is issued before considering any disbursement.
2. Verify that only eligible commodities and acceptable grades (preferably Grade-I) are financed, and reject old, deteriorated, or long-lying stocks.
3. Confirm that the warehouse receipt is issued in the borrower's name and is properly endorsed with clear lien marking in favor of the bank.
4. Conduct mandatory physical verification and sampling to validate quality, quantity, and grade against what is stated on the receipt.
5. Check insurance coverage to ensure stocks are insured for full cost or market value with warehouse location, commodity description, and bank clause incorporated.
6. Insist on updated market valuation and independently verify prevailing commodity prices to prevent inflated valuation.

7. In private or non-WDRA warehouses, ensure compulsory quality checks and Collateral Management Agency oversight as per risk category.
8. Confirm that the warehouse infrastructure, management, and operational controls meet bank standards, including proper pest control and safety measures.
9. Review stock movement procedures to ensure the warehouse will not release any goods without written release orders from the bank.
10. Ensure pledged stock is excluded from CC/OD drawing power calculations to prevent double financing.
11. Establish mark-to-market monitoring and raise timely margin calls for any price drop beyond designated thresholds.
12. Assess borrower integrity and transaction pattern consistency to detect attempts at stock manipulation, substitution, or rapid movement.
13. Ensure the warehouse location is independent of borrower control and avoid inside-mill warehouses unless stringent safeguards and CMAs are deployed.
14. Before first disbursement, confirm that the borrower has demonstrated financial capacity to meet margin calls, warehousing charges, and insurance renewals without dependence on the facility itself.

•••

CASE STUDY 9

THE BANK STATEMENT THAT EXPOSED THE REAL BUSINESS: WHY "BANKING BEHAVIOUR" IS THE MOST HONEST CREDIT DOCUMENT IN UNDERWRITING

1. Introduction

Bank statement analysis has increasingly become the backbone of credit underwriting. Financial statements can be influenced, projections can be optimistic, and GST returns may not always reflect day-to-day liquidity. But a bank statement if obtained completely and interpreted correctly "rarely lies."

The aim of this case is to master the art of detecting risk signals through live banking behaviour: churning, EMI discipline, cheque bounces, electricity consumption patterns, hidden liabilities, and routing of business through multiple accounts.

2. Borrower Background

Borrower Name: M/s Aarav Auto Components (Proprietorship).

Proprietor: Mr. Aarav Malhotra.

Business: Wholesale trading of automobile spare parts for two-wheelers and small commercial vehicles.

Location: Kota Industrial Belt.

Turnover: Approx. ₹5 crore per annum.

Banking Behaviour: Operates two current accounts - one with Union Mercantile Bank (UMB) where limits are proposed, and another with Damodar Commercial Bank (DCB) for collections.

The borrower supplies brake assemblies, clutch plates, filters, and electrical parts to 40 - 50 retailers. The business is moderately working-capital intensive, dependent on continuous stock rotation and steady receivable inflows.

3. Loan / Facility Requested

Type of Facility: Cash Credit (CC) facility.

Amount Requested: ₹75 lakh.

Purpose: Working capital for inventory stocking and receivable cycle.

Collateral: Residential house of proprietor as mortgage.

Secondary Security: Hypothecation of stock and book debts.

4. Key Developments

During appraisal, the credit team flagged multiple banking-related concerns:

Key Findings During Initial Review

i) Credit summation in the primary current account was only 52% of reported sales.

ii) Significant credits were found in another bank account not initially disclosed.

iii) Multiple inward cheque bounces appeared over six months.

iv) The EMI pattern reflected inconsistencies with the borrower's disclosure.

v) Electricity bill payments did not align with the scale of operations claimed.

vi) Interest servicing on an existing small OD facility reflected delays in 2 out of 12 months.

These issues triggered a detailed diagnosis.

5. Detailed Analysis

5.1 Credit Summation / Churning Analysis

The borrower initially submitted only one account i.e. UMB Current Account showing ₹2.6 crore credits over 12 months against reported sales of ₹5 crore (52% summation). As per standard expectations (typically around 75 - 80% churning), the credit team raised an objection.

Upon deeper questioning, the borrower admitted that another current account with DCB was used "only for fast cheque clearing", particularly because many customers operated with that bank.

Action Taken:

- DCB statement collected and analysed.
- Combined summation of UMB + DCB now reflected ₹4.1 crore credits, improving churning to 82%, consistent with industry norms.

This addressed the genuineness of sales but raised strategic concerns:

"Why was the borrower routing the majority of business outside the lending bank?"

The Credit Manager obtained:

i) A written undertaking to route ≥80% of future collections through UMB.

ii) A plan to convert the DCB account into a collection account with T+1 automatic sweeps to UMB.

5.2 Checking for Mid-Period Closed Accounts

Following best-practice instructions from internal guidelines, the Credit Manager also asked whether any account was closed during the analysis period.

The borrower revealed a previously unreported Metro Finance Bank current account, closed in the middle of the year, which also had active transactions earlier. This account was obtained and added to churning analysis to complete the 12-month reconciliation.

5.3 Seasonal / Temporary Delays in Collections

Auto spare parts business experiences mild cyclicity, typically slower collections in monsoon months (June to August).

The analysis period coincided with two slower quarters. To validate delays, a Debtor Reconciliation was performed:

Opening debtors (1 April): ₹42 lakh

Sales during year: ₹5 crore

Total receivables expected: ₹5.42 crore

Realized (credited in banking): ₹4.10 crore

Expected closing debtors: ₹1.32 crore

Borrower's actual debtor list showed ₹1.28 crore, which was a strong match. This supported the argument that lower summation in certain months was due to collection cycle timing, not falsified sales.

5.4 Cheque Bounce Behaviour

Outward bounces: Approximately 18 outward bounces over the year - against 1,200 received cheques (roughly 1.5%), mostly from small retail buyers. These were later adjusted via NEFT/UPI within 3 - 7 days. Acceptable.

Inward bounces: 9 inward bounces across 12 months - more serious, as per internal standards.

Root-Cause Examination:

- 4 bounces were technical: signature mismatch / stale cheque.
- 2 cheques bounced in the morning but cleared the same day, after the borrower deposited funds.
- 3 cheques showed genuine shortfall, all during the monsoon slump.

Using the "percentage approach": Total cheques issued: around 2,500

Genuine inward bounces: 3

Bounce ratio: 0.12% ; Very low.

Thus, while the absolute number seemed high, the effective financial-discipline risk was low.

5.5 EMI & Hidden Liability Detection

The borrower disclosed only two term loans:

a) Small commercial vehicle loan - EMI ₹21,500

b) Housing loan - EMI ₹38,000

During Credit Manager's deep analysis:

- Another EMI of ₹14,950 appeared regularly with narration "ACH Debit RCLFND" not disclosed by the borrower.
- SOA (Statement of Account) was demanded. It revealed a business OD against FD that had slipped into overdue for one month.

This raised two issues: a) Non-disclosure of liability; b) Month-end interest servicing delay, though explained by temporary operating cycle mismatch.

The Manager followed best practices and obtained all SOAs to verify whether: Any EMI bounces occurred, delays were habitual or exceptional and finally any penal interest was levied or not.

5.6 Electricity Consumption - A Powerful Reality Check

Electricity usage often provides an honest, indirect view of a borrower's real operational scale. In this case, the borrower claimed that annual sales had grown from ₹4 crore to ₹5 crore. However, a review of bank statements showed electricity bill payments in the range of ₹11,000 - ₹14,000 per month. Typical for a trading godown, but far too low for any manufacturing or semi-processing activity based of prevailing electricity rates. To verify this, the credit officer obtained two years of electricity bills and examined unit consumption month-wise. The readings showed stable and consistent usage, confirming that the borrower was purely engaged in trading, without any hidden manufacturing or repacking activity. This aligned with the business model of an automobile spare parts wholesaler, where electricity consumption remains relatively flat irrespective of sales growth. Thus, the electricity analysis helped validate the borrower's declared business nature and eliminated concerns regarding inflated turnover or undisclosed production activity.

5.7 Interest Servicing Behaviour - Correct Interpretation

UMB's OD account showed delayed interest servicing in two months.

However:

- In both cases, the account was in credit at the time interest was debited.
- Subsequent deposits were not required for interest clearance.

Please note, If the account has sufficient balance on the date when interest is debited, the interest is considered served regardless of future deposits. This helped close the query around "irregular interest servicing."

6. Outcome / Final Credit Decision

After comprehensive analysis, the credit team concluded:

Positive Indicators

- Combined credit summation of UMB + DCB reached 82%.
- Debtor reconciliation supported sales genuineness.
- Inward cheque bounce ratio extremely low (0.12%).
- Interest servicing delays were technical non-issues.

- Electricity consumption consistent with trading business.
- Borrower provided binding undertaking for routing business through lending bank.

Concerns Mitigated

- Hidden EMI explained and validated.
- DCB account converted into collection account.
- Mid-period closed account reviewed and reconciled.

Final Decision:

CC Limit of ₹75 lakh sanctioned with the following conditions:

i) Minimum 75% monthly business routing through UMB.

ii) Closure / conversion of DCB account into a strictly collection-only account within 60 days.

iii) Quarterly monitoring of cheque bounce trends.

iv) Submission of updated SOAs every six months.

v) Review of debtor ageing >120 days.

The borrower agreed and signed compliance undertakings.

7. Key Lessons for Credit Professionals

i) **Bank statements must be analysed holistically - not account-wise;** summation must be checked across all current accounts, including closed ones.

ii) **Churning mismatches require reconciliation,** not assumptions; debtor analysis can validate delayed collections.

iii) **Inward cheque bounce percentage is the real risk indicator,** not the absolute number of bounce entries.

iv) **EMI entries often reveal hidden liabilities;** always demand SOAs when mismatches arise.

v) **Electricity consumption is a powerful authenticity check,** especially for manufacturing or large-scale trading entities.

v) **Interest servicing must be interpreted correctly** - if interest is debited from a credit balance, the EMI is considered paid even without fresh deposit.

Remember : Credit Summation (Churning)

Credit summation = Total legitimate business inflows visible in bank statements.

High summation indicates: Realised sales, healthy receivable cycle and transparent banking.

Low summation may indicate: Cash sales not deposited, Other-bank routing, Fake/over-invoiced sales, Weak collections.

Bank Statement Analysis Checklist for Credit Professionals

SECTION A — HYGIENE & ACCOUNT SETUP

1. Before any analysis begins, verify that the bank's name, complete account number, borrower name, and address on the statement exactly match the GST certificate, balance sheet, and KYC documents; any mismatch must be explained and recorded.
2. Identify the account type (current, CC, OD, dropline OD, packing credit, savings) and confirm the sanctioned limit and account opening date against the proposal submitted, since each account type demands its own unique focal points of analysis.
3. Review a minimum of 12 months of bank statements to capture a full business cycle, especially for seasonal businesses; a shorter window will distort turnover and repayment behaviour conclusions.

SECTION B — CREDIT SUMMATION / CHURNING

4. Compute credit summation only after filtering out loan disbursements, OD/CC drawdowns, inter-account self-transfers, sister-concern transfers, FD sweep-in/sweep-out credits, and personal/non-business receipts; totalling all credits blindly will grossly overstate true turnover.
5. Apply the 80% routing benchmark: for a normal B2B non-cash-intensive business, at least 80% of reported sales should be visible as genuine business credits in the bank for the same period; deviations exceeding 20–25% must be documented with evidence, not just verbal explanation.
6. Cross-check bank credits against the top 40–50 debtors from the latest balance sheet; if major customers or their financiers (e.g., Bajaj Finance)

are consistently absent from credit narrations, treat it as a serious red flag on the genuineness of reported sales.

7. When credits appear from third-party financiers (NBFCs, banks) instead of the buyer's name, obtain documentary mapping (invoice copy, financing arrangement, or ledger extract) to confirm these are genuine invoice settlements and not fresh loans to the borrower.
8. Any unusually large credit entry that significantly exceeds the normal invoice ticket size of the business must be individually verified with invoices, contracts, or ledger extracts before being treated as regular operating turnover.
9. When credit summation is low, always check whether the borrower operated any additional or now-closed current accounts during the analysis period; collections routed through those accounts must be consolidated before concluding on actual churning.
10. For borrowers who collect through another bank's current account, either obtain an undertaking to close or convert it into a collection account with auto-sweep to the lending bank, or use the alternate statement to first prove genuineness of collections before addressing the routing concern.

SECTION C — DEBIT SUMMATION & PURCHASE VERIFICATION

11. On the debit side, isolate only supplier-related payment outflows and reconcile them with purchase bills, invoices, and inventory records; if the borrower claims heavy procurement but no corresponding supplier debits exist, it is a direct red flag on purchase authenticity.
12. When debit-side analysis reveals suppliers not appearing in GST data (unregistered or small vendors), rely on the bank statement as the primary reconciliation tool since GST does not capture such transactions.
13. Maintain a tolerance framework for debit-side reconciliation: a variance of 5–10% between reported purchases and banked supplier payments is acceptable; mismatches of 20–25% or more demand escalation and documentary evidence from the borrower.

SECTION D — EMI & LOAN REPAYMENT ANALYSIS

14. Before matching EMIs in the bank statement, compile a complete loan inventory from four sources (client submission, sanction letters/ repayment schedules, balance sheet liabilities, and individual + commercial

CIBIL) and build an Excel tracker of all running loans, EMI amounts, and due dates.

15. If an EMI falls due on a bank/public holiday and is debited the next working day, do not classify it as a delay; always cross-reference a calendar before marking any EMI as late.
16. When an EMI is missing for a specific month, check the closing balance the day before the due date; if the balance was insufficient, treat it as a probable bounce and demand the Statement of Account (SOA) from the lending institution to confirm actual debit date, penal interest, and overdue status.
17. Never accept a repayment schedule as proof of actual payment history; a schedule is only a future plan, whereas the SOA records actual debits, bounces, penal charges, and overdue dates from disbursement to date and constitutes the only reliable evidence of repayment behaviour.
18. Identify EMIs paid through ACH/ECS mandates by scanning narrations for "ECS," "ACH," "Auto Debit," or "Loan Repayment"; for cheque-based EMIs, focus on the 1st–10th of each month and flag recurring identical amounts on similar dates across consecutive months as likely EMI candidates.
19. Where a lender debits interest and principal separately (common in government banks), add both components to calculate the effective monthly EMI and verify the combined pattern month-on-month.
20. If recurring debit amounts appear via ACH/ECS that cannot be matched to any declared loan in CIBIL, balance sheet, or client disclosures, treat them as hidden liabilities and investigate the lender and facility type before proceeding with underwriting.
21. When personal loan EMIs (e.g., housing loan) of the proprietor are being paid from the firm's current account, quantify the annual capital withdrawal impact and re-assess leverage, gearing, and current ratios after deducting personal residential property from business capital.

SECTION E — ELECTRICITY & UTILITY AS PRODUCTION PROXY

22. For manufacturing borrowers, track month-wise electricity bill payments from the bank statement and compare the payment trend against the claimed growth in sales; flat or declining electricity outflows alongside

rising sales should trigger a deeper enquiry into whether the growth is genuinely production-led or driven by trading or price inflation.

23. Go beyond rupee amounts in electricity analysis: request bill copies for two comparable months across years and extract unit consumption (kWh), since tariff rates can change and unit consumption is the more reliable proxy for actual production volume.
24. When a borrower pays electricity bills via credit card (common for cashback benefits), the bank statement will reflect "Credit Card Payment" rather than a direct electricity board debit; in such cases, obtain the credit card statement or bill copies to confirm and quantify the actual power expense.

SECTION F — CHEQUE BOUNCE ANALYSIS

25. Distinguish clearly between inward and outward cheque bounces: inward bounces (borrower's own cheques to suppliers returned unpaid) indicate the borrower's inability to honour payment obligations and are high-risk; outward bounces (customers' cheques deposited by the borrower that return) reflect the customer's financial weakness and are relatively less severe.
26. Calculate bounce percentage on a volumetric basis (total bounced cheques divided by total cheques issued or received across all accounts) rather than judging by absolute count; up to 2–3% is generally tolerable with strong justifications, while 7–8% or above is a serious red flag.
27. Exclude from the bounce count all cheques that were bounced and cleared on the same day, and all technical bounces (signature mismatch, stale date, words–figures mismatch, wrong account number) since these do not reflect fund shortfalls.
28. Analyse the date pattern of genuine bounces: if most bounces cluster on one or two isolated dates in the year rather than recurring monthly, treat them as exceptional operational mismanagement events rather than evidence of structural cash flow stress, and verify whether all dues were cleared within a few days afterward.
29. For inward bounces where sufficient balance existed in another account of the same bank, or where there was significant unutilised CC/OD drawing power on the bounce date, treat the incident as funds mis-management

by the accountant rather than borrower insolvency; a bank error letter or unutilised-limit evidence strengthens this argument significantly.

SECTION G — ADVANCED RED FLAGS & PATTERN CHECKS

30. Flag accounts that consistently run near-zero closing balances, show frequent large round-figure transactions, or exhibit large credits immediately reversed within one to two days; these patterns indicate tight liquidity, accommodation entries, or fund cycling and must be investigated before sanctioning limits.
31. Treat RTGS/NEFT/IMPS return entries distinctly from cheque bounces; electronic transfer rejections typically arise from insufficient balance at the moment of initiation or incorrect details and are primarily operational errors, not evidence of deliberate payment default or financial indiscipline.

Please Remember: Bank statements are the most tamper-resistant evidence in MSME underwriting. Read narrations, reconcile both sides, verify counterparties, respect seasonality, and let behavioural data override reported financials when the two conflict.

•••

CASE STUDY 10

THE OFF-SEASON STOCK SPIKE THAT SHOULD SCARE ANY CREDIT HEAD

Triangulating stock statements with collections to detect inflated receivables and DP padding

1. Introduction

Agro-based units often operate in cycles with heavy procurement during harvest, gradual processing, and sales spread across the year. Because stock levels fluctuate sharply, monthly stock statements become the most powerful tool for a credit manager to verify the health of the business. This case examines how a bank uncovered early warning signals in a rural agro-processing borrower through inconsistencies in stock statements, leading to a timely corrective decision.

2. Borrower / Business Background

M/s GreenHarvest Agro Mills, based in the outskirts of Meerut (Uttar Pradesh), processes raw sugarcane into jaggery and refined sugar. The unit is run by proprietor Mr. Raghav Verma, who has 15+ years of experience in the agro-processing sector.

Key business details:

- Product line: Raw jaggery blocks, powdered jaggery, refined brown sugar.
- Installed capacity: 18 MT/day.
- Seasonal procurement: November - March.
- Annual turnover: ₹28 - 32 crore (season-dependent).
- Major customers: Wholesalers in UP, MP, and Rajasthan.
- Accounting is done by an external consultant; no ERP system in place.
- No collateral offered other than hypothecation of current assets.

3. Type of Loan / Facility Details

The borrower enjoys the following working capital facility with Bharat General Bank (BGB):

- Cash Credit (₹4.50 crore) against stock + book debts.
- Margin: Raw Materials - 35% , WIP - 40%, Finished Goods - 25%, Book Debts (≤90 days) - 25%.
- Stock statement submission by 10th of every month.
- DP to be calculated on paid stock basis (stock minus creditors).

4. Scenario

For the first two years, account conduct remained normal with average utilisation at ~75% of limits. However, during the last renewal cycle, the credit officer noticed unusual patterns:

i) Stock levels showed steep month-on-month increases despite the off-season.

ii) Creditor levels jumped significantly, resulting in negative paid stock for two consecutive months.

iii) Book debts increased sharply but bank account credits did not reflect corresponding sales realisation.

iv) GST returns displayed lower outward supplies compared to sales shown in the stock statement.

v) Stock with job-workers was suddenly introduced in the stock statement without prior intimation or documentation.

5. Problem Statement

a) Stock levels reported during the off-season were disproportionately high and inconsistent with the production cycle of an agro-processing unit, indicating possible overvaluation or window dressing.

b) Creditor balances exceeded stock value for multiple months, resulting in negative paid stock and suggesting that bank funds were likely diverted away from working capital needs.

c) Sales and debtor figures declared in the stock statement failed to reconcile with GST filings and bank account credits, raising concerns about inflated receivables and potential unreported sales routed outside the banking channel.

d) A sudden introduction of stock with job-workers without supporting challans, registers, or audit trails created doubts about the authentication of reported inventory and the possibility of double financing or misclassification.

6. Detailed Analysis

The credit team undertook a multi-layered review of GreenHarvest Agro Mills' operations, numbers, and compliance behaviour. What emerged was not just a few inconsistencies, it was a pattern of structural stress, signalling that the borrower's reported financial position did not reflect the true on-ground situation.

Seasonality vs. Reported Stock Behaviour

For agro-processing units dependent on sugarcane, the production cycle is predictable. Raw material availability peaks from November to March, followed by tapering inventory and higher sales during summer. Yet, the borrower's stock statements showed an unexplained 40 - 45% rise in inventory during June - September, which is counterintuitive.

A seasoned credit professional knows that:

- Off-season stock should normally reduce, not grow.
- Any upward movement must be justified by forward sales contracts or confirmed orders.
- Excessive finished goods in off-season may indicate forced holding, slow-moving inventory, or paper-based stock inflation.

This mismatch between operational logic and financial reporting was the first major red flag.

Negative Paid Stock and the Liquidity Paradox

Paid stock after deducting trade creditors is the true security available for bank financing. When creditors consistently exceed stock, it means:

- Suppliers are funding working capital, not the bank.
- Bank funds may be deployed elsewhere like fixed assets, related parties, or circular transactions.
- Borrower may be delaying payments to creditors to maintain cash flow liquidity.

For GreenHarvest, two consecutive months of negative paid stock indicated a liquidity inversion. The company had created an image of abundant stock, but the ownership of this stock (economically) belonged to suppliers. This revealed underlying stress and potential diversion of bank funds.

Debtors vs. Bank Credits vs. GST

A professional credit analysis demands this triangulation test. When numbers don't match across independent data sources, reliability collapses. The borrower reported a surge in debtors from ₹1.80 crore to ₹2.95 crore within two months. However:

- Bank credits remained flat, showing no increase in collections.
- GST outward supplies were lower, indicating that sales were overstated in stock statements.
- Debtor ageing was inconsistent, with many accounts showing unrealistically long cycles for the agro-trade industry.

This indicated one of the following:

- Inflation of receivables to boost Drawing Power.
- Routing of sales through other undisclosed bank accounts.
- Sale-on-cash terms that were not reflected in the CC account.
- Potential related-party sales without actual collection.

For credit professionals, such mismatches are often early signs of stress migration, a precursor to account slippage.

Questionable WIP and Job-Worker Stock Entries

The borrower suddenly reported significant stock lying with job-workers (₹38 lakh) for the first time in several years. Such entries require: Job-work challans, Dispatch records, Returnable gate passes, Job-worker registers, Matching consumption and output ratios.

But, None were available.

In agro-based processing, job-work inventory is rare unless supported by a specific outsourcing arrangement. The sudden emergence of this category suggested:

- Misclassification to inflate eligible stock.
- Possible double financing through related job-workers.
- Attempted accommodation entries to fill stock gaps.

For the bank, this raised concerns about the physical existence and ownership of reported inventory.

The Drawing Power Reality Check

When the credit team recalculated DP using bank-approved eligibility rules:

- Ineligible stock was removed.
- Stock with job-workers was excluded.
- Debtors above 90 days were disallowed.
- Excessive creditors were adjusted.
- Higher margins were applied to liquidate doubts.

The true eligible DP shrank to ₹2.76 crore against the ₹4.32 crore outstanding. This was not a minor discrepancy, in fact, it was a structural breach.

Under RBI's IRAC norms, such persistent irregularity (outstanding > DP beyond 90 days) can trigger SMA-2 status and eventual NPA classification unless corrected. The case had moved from operational inconsistency to risk classification threat.

Operational Controls - What the Ground Reality Revealed?

Physical verification visits indicated:

- Improper stock registers.
- Irregular updating of production logs.
- No internal reconciliation between book stock and physical stock.
- Insurance cover lower than reported stock levels.
- No hypothecation boards at secondary godowns.

Such weak operating controls often correlate with financial manipulation and inadequate governance. For agro-based units, which already face price volatility, weak internal controls amplify credit risk significantly.

7. Outcome / Final Decision

The credit committee concluded that the borrower's data was unreliable and that the risk of diversion of funds could not be ignored. The following actions were taken:

a) DP was restricted strictly based on recomputed eligibility.

b) Borrower was asked to route 100% sales through the CC account, failing which DP would be further reduced.

c) A stock audit was ordered, prioritising verification of job-worker stock and physical tally.

d) Until stock audit completion, clear instructions were issued to freeze enhancements, avoid ad-hoc limits, and control any further drawings.

e) Based on the audit's adverse findings, the bank downgraded the account to Special Mention Account-2 (SMA-2) and initiated a structured exit by asking the borrower to arrange takeover or reduction of limits.

f) The borrower eventually shifted to a co-operative bank with looser monitoring norms, enabling BGB to safely reduce exposure without incurring loss.

8. Key Lessons for Credit Professionals

a) Stock statement trend analysis is the most reliable early-warning tool, especially in seasonal agro-based units where manipulation is easier.

b) Negative paid stock is a powerful red flag indicating diversion or over-dependence on supplier credit.

c) Always reconcile stock statements with GST returns, bank credits, and production logic; inconsistencies often reveal hidden stress.

d) Stock with job-workers must never be accepted without documentary proof, as it is a common channel for misreporting and double financing.

Stock-Statement Checklist for Credit Managers

1. Ensure the stock statement is submitted within the stipulated timeline (usually within 7–15 days of month-end) to avoid reliance on outdated data.
2. Verify that the statement corresponds exactly to the month-end date and not to a mid-month or arbitrary date.

3. Check whether quantity, value, and rate columns are correctly filled and mathematically consistent.
4. Confirm that stock values are reported at cost or lower of cost/market as per bank policy.
5. Reconcile opening stock with previous month's closing stock to detect manipulation or data inconsistency.
6. Scrutinize abnormal month-on-month fluctuations in raw material, WIP, or finished goods and seek explanations.
7. Ensure that obsolete, non-moving, damaged, or slow-moving stock is identified and treated as ineligible.
8. Verify the accuracy of paid stock by deducting trade creditors and ensuring only genuine trade creditors are considered.
9. Examine whether the inventory mix (raw material vs. WIP vs. finished goods) aligns with the business's operational cycle.
10. Confirm that goods shown as "in transit" or "with job workers" are supported by proper challans and documentary evidence.
11. Validate that book debts shown for DP calculation have a proper ageing statement and comply with the permitted age norms.
12. Cross-check sales and purchase trends in GST returns to ensure consistency with stock movement and debtor/creditor levels.
13. Recalculate Drawing Power independently and compare it with branch DP to identify errors or overstatements.
14. Confirm that insured stock value is adequate and the bank clause is correctly incorporated in the policy.
15. Review stock audit observations, if applicable, and ensure that all adverse comments have been addressed.
16. Compare stock levels with bank credit summations to verify that reported sales translate into actual bank inflows.
17. Assess whether job-worker stock quantities genuinely reflect processing capacity and not fictitious entries.
18. Ensure that no fixed assets, tools, machinery, or capital items are wrongly included under stock.

19. Verify whether creditors are increasing disproportionately, which may indicate liquidity stress or diversion of funds.
20. Match physical verification findings with reported stock levels to validate that the primary security actually exists.
21. Always check whether stock and debtor levels rise sharply near renewal dates, as this is a classic window-dressing pattern.
22. Review whether the borrower uses multiple bank accounts for routing sales proceeds, which can distort stock–to–churning relationships.
23. Evaluate whether sudden spikes in WIP correlate with realistic consumption ratios; unusually high WIP often signals value-padding.

•••

CASE STUDY 11

WHEN THE NUMBERS LOOK RIGHT BUT THE GST STORY DOESN'T

Spotting sales inflation, reporting inconsistency, and the real meaning of repeated mismatches

1. Introduction

In the post-GST lending environment, a borrower's real business activity can be assessed more reliably from monthly GSTR-1, GSTR-3B and GSTR-2B than from conventional audited financials. For trading units, like pharma distributors, GST returns offer direct visibility into sales velocity, purchase patterns, cash-flow discipline and vendor quality.

This case study examines a working capital enhancement request by a mid-sized pharma distributor where financial statements appeared stable, but GST analytics revealed a more refined picture requiring deeper credit judgement.

2. Borrower / Business Background

Borrower: Medisphere Pharma Distributors.

Promoter: Mr. Abhinav Khatri (Age 42, B.Com).

Location: Pune, Maharashtra.

Nature of Business: Wholesale distribution of branded pharmaceutical products to hospitals, clinics and retail chemists.

Product Basket: Antibiotics, OTC pain relievers, paediatric formulations, injectables, consumables.

Operating Model: High-volume, thin-margin trading (typical margin 3–8%).

Years of Existence: 11

GST Scheme: Regular monthly filer.

GSTINs: Two - Maharashtra (main), Karnataka (secondary depot).

3. Type of Loan / Facility Details

Existing Facility: Cash Credit (₹1.50 crore).

Requested Enhancement: Additional ₹1.00 crore (Total CC: ₹2.50 crore).

Purpose: To support increased inventory stocking for expanded hospital supply contracts.

Security: Hypothecation of stock & book debts; collateral: residential property.

Banking Conduct: Generally satisfactory; occasional overdrawals adjusted within 2-3 days.

4. Major Developments

The borrower projected a business expansion due to onboarding three medium-sized hospitals in Pune and Bangalore.

Audited FY statements reflected a topline of ₹14.2 crore with moderate profitability. At face value, the business seemed stable, with reasonable stock levels and acceptable debtor ageing. However, the bank mandated deep GST-led analysis for consistency, verification, and fraud-risk mitigation. This required triangulating GSTR-1, GSTR-3B and GSTR-2B with bank statements, stock reports and CMA data, as recommended across modern credit frameworks.

The GST-based evaluation revealed multiple technical inconsistencies requiring professional scrutiny.

5. Problem Statement

a) GSTR-1 and GSTR-3B mismatched in most months, indicating inconsistent sales reporting and potential overstatement of outward supplies.

b) Cash GST payment remained unusually low, raising doubts about value addition, genuine purchases, and ITC quality.

c) GSTR-2B showed repeated supplier non-compliance, exposing the borrower to ITC blockage and cash-flow risk.

d) Declared stock-statement sales exceeded GST turnover, suggesting possible inflation of current assets or routing of sales outside GST.

e) CMA-projected growth far exceeded GST trends, casting doubt on the credibility and sustainability of projected turnover.

6. Detailed Analysis

6.1 GSTR-1 vs GSTR-3B Reconciliation

A review of 12-month data showed GSTR-1 outward supplies consistently higher than taxable turnover declared in GSTR-3B in 8 out of 12 months.

In a trading business, this gap should be minimal, because both returns arise from the same invoices.

Persistent differences can signal: delayed reporting of credit notes, errors in taxable value reporting, or intentional inflation of GSTR-1 to appear larger to counterparties.

6.2 Cash vs ITC Utilisation

The borrower reported less than 2% cash tax payment for most months.

In pharma trading, input and output GST rates generally match (12% and 18%), hence traders rely heavily on ITC, but still end up with some positive cash liability due to: higher-margin items, service inputs without ITC, or timing differences.

Industry expectations usually show 1 - 5% cash outflow, but zero or near-zero cash tax for long periods may indicate: heavy dependence on suppliers filing on time, over-reporting of purchase value, or potential circular invoicing risks (red flag noted across GST forensic frameworks).

6.3 GSTR-2B Vendor Compliance Issues

GSTR-2B reflected multiple invoices marked as “Not Eligible” or “Deferred”, indicating that several suppliers either did not file GSTR-1 on time or filed incorrect returns.

Since ITC is vendor-dependent, any blockage directly affects the borrower’s working capital.

Poor-quality vendors also imply: business disruption risk, credit impact due to delayed ITC or future tax disputes and demand risk (tax + interest + penalty).

Vendor compliance is a strong predictor of borrower riskiness in GST-led credit underwriting.

6.4 Turnover vs Stock Statements

The borrower's monthly stock statements showed ₹1.2 - 1.5 crore sales, but GST turnover data averaged ₹95 - 110 lakh. Such divergence (20-30%) may result from:

- inflated sales declared for DP purposes,
- bulk purchases booked but slow actual sales,
- cash sales not reflected in GST returns, or
- GSTR-1 errors (unlikely because pharma invoices are automated).

As per best practice, credit officers must rely on GST sales as the real turnover proxy rather than unverified stock statements.

6.5 GST Trend vs CMA Projections

GST turnover had grown 5-7% YoY, but the CMA projected 35% growth based on expected new hospital contracts. Growth projections must align with historical GST performance unless strong documentary evidence exists. As per modern underwriting principles, GST trendlines must anchor realistic sales projections, not aggressive promoter assumptions.

7. Outcome / Final Decision

After comprehensive review, the bank decided not to grant the full enhancement and instead approved a partial enhancement of ₹50 lakh, subject to strict conditions.

Conditions Imposed:

a) Monthly submission of GSTR-1, GSTR-3B and GSTR-2B, verified through GSTN API access.
b) Reduction of supplier dependency risk: borrower to replace non-compliant vendors within 3 months.
c) Submission of hospital contracts and evidence of actual order flow before any future enhancement.
d) Drawing Power to be calculated based on GST turnover, not stock statement turnover.
e) Limit review if GSTR-1 vs GSTR-3B mismatch exceeds 10% for two consecutive months.

Rationale- The borrower demonstrated stable fundamentals, but the GST-led anomalies reduced reliability of projected business expansion.

A moderate enhancement balanced business need with bank's prudential risk management.

8. Key Lessons for Credit Professionals

a) Always verify turnover through GSTR-3B taxable value rather than audited financials or stock statements.

b) Watch for persistent GSTR-1 and GSTR-3B mismatches; they are early indicators of inflated or inconsistent reporting.

c) Evaluate vendor quality using GSTR-2B - weak supplier compliance directly threatens borrower liquidity.

d) Use GST trends to validate CMA projections; unrealistic growth projections must be challenged.

e) For trading units, near-zero cash tax payment over long periods requires deep scrutiny of value addition and purchase behaviour.

GST-Based Credit Appraisal Checklist for Credit Managers

1. Verify whether all GSTR-1 and GSTR-3B returns are filed on time for the last 12 months to assess compliance discipline.
2. Compare outward supplies in GSTR-1 with taxable turnover in GSTR-3B to detect mismatches or inflated sales.
3. Check the consistency of ITC utilisation in GSTR-3B and ensure cash tax payment levels are appropriate for the borrower's value-addition model.
4. Examine GSTR-2B for supplier compliance and identify invoices marked as ineligible or not reflected due to vendor non-filing.
5. Cross-verify monthly GST sales with bank credit summations to ensure reported turnover is actually routed through banking channels.
6. Review the Electronic Cash Ledger for patterns of timely tax payment and cash flow behaviour.
7. Inspect the Electronic Credit Ledger to identify unusual accumulation of ITC that may signal stockpiling or bogus billing.
8. Examine the Liability Register for past demands, penalties, or unresolved tax disputes that may affect borrower liquidity.
9. Identify credit notes issued (GST vs financial) to distinguish between genuine returns and commercial adjustments impacting real turnover.

10. Reconcile annual GST turnover (GSTR-9) with audited financials to identify timing differences, stock transfers, or unbilled revenue gaps.
11. Analyse HSN summaries in GSTR-1 to confirm that the borrower's declared business line matches its actual product profile.
12. Evaluate customer concentration using GSTR-1 buyer-wise data to identify dependence on a few GSTINs.
13. Review GSTR-2B supplier data for vendor concentration and potential exposure to non-compliant or high-risk suppliers.
14. Compare GST-derived purchase values with stock statements to identify inflated inventory or manipulated DP declarations.
15. Assess whether projections in CMA data align with 12-month GST trendlines, not just management assumptions.
16. Identify inter-state stock transfers across multiple GSTINs and ensure they are adjusted correctly when evaluating turnover.
17. Analyse ITC mismatch patterns that may indicate circular trading or shell-vendor activity.
18. Track the ratio of taxable output to taxable input to assess gross margin behaviour and detect red flags in value addition.
19. Check if the borrower belongs to sectors with inverted duty structures and evaluate refund dependency risk.
20. Review QRMP or Composition scheme taxpayers separately to ensure correct interpretation of their GST filings.
21. Use GST data to validate realistic working capital cycles by correlating purchases, sales, and tax utilisation patterns.
22. Check the timing of GST payments against bank statements to ensure tax payments are genuinely flowing from business operations and not from temporary borrowings.
23. Evaluate month-on-month fluctuations in GSTR-3B liability to detect abnormal spikes that may indicate end-of-year adjustment billing.
24. Flag any consistent delays in vendor reporting in GSTR-2B as early warning signals for future ITC reversals affecting borrower liquidity.
25. Assess whether the borrower's GST behaviour aligns with industry benchmarks to detect operational irregularities or revenue smoothing.

•••

CASE STUDY 12

FOIR VS "BLACK INCOME": HOW AN AUTO LOAN TOP-UP FOR A PROPRIETOR NEARLY BECAME A DEBT TRAP

1. Introduction

This case explores the dilemma faced by a mid-sized private sector bank while assessing an auto loan and top-up request from a sole proprietor engaged in road transport.

The case highlights how over-reliance on "black income", pressure to meet business targets, and incomplete recognition of obligations can push Fixed Obligation to Income Ratio (FOIR) beyond safe limits, especially in proprietor-driven businesses, and why disciplined FOIR-based underwriting is critical in auto and other income-based loans.

2. Borrower / Business Background

The borrower is M/s Shree Ganesh Roadlines, a proprietorship firm owned by Mr. Rohan Deshpande, based in the transport hub of Kolhapur. The firm has been in operation for around seven years, providing point-to-point freight services for FMCG distributors and small manufacturers in a 300 - 400 km radius.

The business model is typical of small fleet operators:

i) Four medium commercial vehicles (MCVs) financed by an NBFC and another bank.

ii) One small car used partly for business marketing and partly for family use.

iii) High proportion of freight receipts in cash, especially from smaller clients, with partial banking of collections.

As per the last two years' income tax returns, the firm reported:

i) Turnover in the range of ₹1.8 - 2.1 crore.

ii) Profit after tax averaging around ₹15 lakh per annum, implying usable monthly income of about ₹1.20 lakh, after normalising for non-cash and non-recurring items.

Mr. Deshpande lives in a joint family and is perceived locally as a hardworking, hands-on businessman. However, his financial discipline is mixed: some delays in loan EMI payments have occurred during lean seasons, and a few short-term borrowings from NBFCs and gold loans were used to manage cash flow gaps.

3. Type of Loan / Facility Details

The case arises when Mr. Deshpande approaches Sahyadri Bank Ltd. with the following requirements:

a) **New Auto Loan** for purchase of a fifth medium commercial vehicle:
  - Vehicle Cost (on-road): approximately ₹22 lakh.
  - Proposed Loan: ₹18 lakh.
  - Proposed Tenure: 5 years.
  - Security: Hypothecation of the new vehicle, along with personal guarantee of the proprietor.

b) **Top-Up on Existing Auto** Loan with the same bank:
  - Existing Auto Loan (for a 3-year old vehicle) - current EMI: ₹26,000 per month
  - Requested Top-Up: ₹2 lakh, to be structured through enhancement of the existing loan, resulting in an increase of EMI by about ₹4,000 per month

The sales team positions the total proposal as a "wallet-deepening" opportunity: growing transport business, repeat customer, secured lending, and strong local relationships. As per bank policy, auto loans to proprietors are assessed primarily on FOIR, along with bureau score and banking behaviour, even though the underlying cash flows arise from business operations.

4. Major Developments

At the branch, the relationship manager prepares an initial eligibility assessment based on the customer's verbal declaration of income and obligations. Mr. Deshpande states that his actual monthly income is ₹2.0 - 2.2 lakh, but admits that only around ₹1.2 lakh is visible in ITR and bank statements; the rest is cash balance and off-the-books freight.

He also mentions that his spouse runs a small home-based boutique generating about ₹40,000 per month in cash, for which no ITR or formal accounts are available. He expects the bank to consider this additional income for FOIR, arguing that "actual affordability" is far better than the documents show.

The initial FOIR working, prepared casually at the sourcing stage, takes total income as ₹1.9 lakh (combining declared income, estimated cash business income, and spouse's boutique income), and lists only two visible EMIs: i) Existing auto loan with Sahyadri Bank: ₹26,000 per month; ii) One NBFC truck loan: ₹24,000 per month.

Ignoring other obligations and relying on inflated income, the sourcing sheet shows FOIR at around 26% post-sanction which was appearing comfortably within the internal cap of 60% for this risk segment.

However, once the file reaches the credit manager, the story begins to unravel. A detailed review of CIBIL report, bank statements, and loan documents reveals a different picture:

- Two existing commercial vehicle EMIs: ₹26,000 and ₹24,000.
- A car loan EMI of ₹9,000.
- A gold loan with structured monthly repayment of ₹4,000.
- A credit card with average outstanding of about ₹60,000, where policy requires loading either 5% of limit or outstanding as a notional EMI, taken here as ₹3,000 per month
- Past delays of 30+ days in repayment of the NBFC vehicle loan and one settled consumer durable loan from four years ago, depressing the bureau score to around 685

As the true obligations surface, the real FOIR starts moving dangerously towards the top of the policy range.

5. Problem Statement

a) Whether FOIR remains within policy once all fixed obligations, including NBFC loans, gold loan and credit card exposure, are correctly identified and loaded against only documented, verifiable income.

b) Whether unverified cash earnings and spouse's undocumented business income can be justifiably considered for FOIR to support a borderline auto loan and top-up request, without violating responsible lending standards and internal audit expectations.

c) How to decide on the new auto loan and top-up in light of a moderate bureau score, past delinquencies and visible signs of over-leveraging, while managing business pressure to approve a seemingly "secured" proposal.

6. Detailed Analysis

6.1 Correct FOIR Framework – Income vs Fixed Obligations

By definition, FOIR measures what percentage of a borrower's net monthly income is already committed to fixed monthly obligations such as EMIs and mandated repayments. The formula is:

FOIR = (Total Fixed Monthly Obligations / Net Monthly Income) × 100

For a proprietor, "net monthly income" should be derived from audited or ITR-based business results, normalised drawings, and supported by banking records, not from unverifiable cash claims. FOIR is designed as a conservative affordability tool, unlike DSCR which can incorporate projected future business performance.

In this case, the credit manager decides to rely on:

i) Average profit after tax from the last two ITRs: about ₹15 lakh per year.

ii) Normalised usable income (after reasonable adjustments): ₹1.20 lakh per month.

Spouse's boutique income is treated only as a qualitative comfort, not loaded into FOIR, as there are neither tax returns nor clear banking evidence.

6.2 Recognition of Global Fixed Obligations

Next, the credit manager reconstructs the complete obligation picture from bureau and statements:

i) Existing Auto Loan – Sahyadri Bank: ₹26,000.

ii) MCV Loan – NBFC: ₹24,000.

iii) Car Loan – NBFC: ₹9,000.

iv) Gold Loan – NBFC: ₹4,000.

v) Credit Card – notional EMI: ₹3,000.

Total existing fixed obligations = ₹66,000 per month. On this basis, current FOIR before the proposed loan is: 66,000 / 1,20,000 = 55%

This is already at the upper end of the bank's comfort band of 50 - 60% for self-employed, transport segment borrowers. With the proposed new auto loan EMI of about ₹38,000 and a top-up EMI increase of ₹4,000, the total obligations become:

- Existing obligations: ₹66,000.
- Incremental EMI: ₹42,000.
- Total post-sanction obligations: ₹1,08,000.

Post-sanction FOIR would be: 1,08,000 / 1,20,000 = 90%

A FOIR of 90% effectively means that only 10% of documented income is left to meet all household and business living expenses, fuel, maintenance, education, medical costs and contingencies. From a risk perspective, this is clearly unsustainable.

6.3 The "Black Income" Argument

Mr. Deshpande strongly argues that this FOIR is "unfair" because it ignores: i) Significant unreported cash freight receipts in the business, and ii) His spouse's boutique cash income.

He insists that if "actual" income of around ₹2 lakh per month is considered, FOIR would fall to nearly 54% (₹1,08,000 / ₹2,00,000), which is within policy.

However, modern credit practice clearly warns against relying on unsubstantiated income, especially when sanctioning long-tenor loans based on EMI repayment from "white money". FOIR is meant to be a white-income-based affordability ratio, and while many lenders in the market stretch FOIR to very high levels, sometimes even 150 - 200%, by informally assuming black income, this approach greatly increases default risk and is not aligned with prudent, audit-proof lending standards.

The credit manager concludes that:

i) Only verifiable income (ITR, financial statements, bank credits, etc.) can be used in FOIR;

ii) Unreported cash flows may be considered as soft comfort but cannot be the basis for sanction in a regulated bank.

6.4 DSCR vs FOIR – Why "Business Can Pay" is Not Enough

The relationship manager attempts another line of argument: based on projected freight contracts and expected business growth, the Debt Service Coverage Ratio (DSCR) for the business appears comfortable at around 1.35x, assuming higher turnover next year.

However, this misses the critical conceptual distinction:

i) DSCR is primarily a business cash-flow tool, focusing on whether the business can generate sufficient funds to service term loans over a period, often using projections.

ii) FOIR is a personal / household affordability tool, particularly for retail and proprietor-driven loans, measuring how much of the proprietor's documented income is locked into fixed obligations at a point in time.

In this auto loan, the bank's board-approved retail credit policy clearly prescribes FOIR-based eligibility. Even if DSCR appears acceptable on optimistic projections, the current FOIR of 90% on documented income signposts serious over-leverage at the personal level.

6.5 Bureau Behaviour and Early Warning Signals

The bureau report adds further caution:

i) Past 30+ DPDs on the NBFC truck loan in two instances.

ii) One settled consumer durable loan from four years earlier.

iii) Current score around 685, below the internal "sweet spot" for a high-FOIR sanction.

Taken together with a FOIR of 90%, these are strong early warning indicators of stress. RBI's emphasis on responsible lending, fair practices, and board-approved risk appetite requires banks to avoid pushing borrowers into unsustainable EMI burdens merely to grow portfolio size.

6.6 Evaluating Possible Mitigants

The credit manager explores various options:

i) **Reducing the loan amount** or extending the tenure to bring EMI down. However, even a significantly lower EMI still keeps FOIR well above 70% on the same documented income.

ii) **Adding a salaried co-borrower** with strong documented income, but in this case no such family member with clean income and bureau profile is available.

iii) **Insisting on closure of one existing NBFC truck loan** from own sources before sanction. This reduces obligations, but the borrower does not have the required margin and is relying on the top-up itself for liquidity.

Ultimately, the mitigants are either impractical or insufficient to bring FOIR within the 50–60% band in a manner that is both policy-compliant and defensible before internal audit and regulators.

7. Outcome / Final Decision

After detailed discussion with the branch, business head and risk team, the credit manager recommends the following:

a) Reject the request for the new auto loan and the top-up in its present form, citing FOIR breach, high leverage, and bureau behaviour not commensurate with the proposed obligations.

b) Clearly document the FOIR working on both existing and proposed basis, the income rationale, recognition of all obligations, and the reasons for not considering unverified cash income.

c) Offer the customer a future re-evaluation after at least 12 months of clean repayment conduct on existing loans and better documentation of income (including bringing more business into banking channels and filing higher, realistic ITRs).

d) Encourage the branch to maintain the relationship through transactional banking, but not to dilute FOIR norms for short-term volume gains.

The recommendation is approved by the sanctioning authority. The decision is communicated to the borrower transparently, emphasising concern for his long-term financial stability and the bank's obligation to lend responsibly.

8. Key Lessons for Credit Professionals

a) FOIR is a conservative, white-income-based affordability tool and must be calculated strictly on verifiable income and all fixed obligations; using unsubstantiated cash or "black income" to justify a sanction defeats its risk-control purpose.

b) In proprietor-driven businesses, always adopt a "Global FOIR" view, combining all personal and business-linked obligations appearing in CIBIL, bank statements and loan documents, before deciding on any new auto, LAP or personal loan exposure.

c) Do not let a comfortable projected DSCR or perceived business potential override a clearly stressed FOIR; DSCR assesses business cash flow, while FOIR protects household-level repayment capacity and is critical in income-based retail underwriting.

d) When FOIR approaches or breaches policy thresholds in the presence of bureau issues and multiple NBFC exposures, the safest and most professional decision is often to decline or significantly scale down the proposal, fully documenting the rationale for future audit and portfolio reviews.

•••

CASE STUDY 13

THE INFLATED DP TRAP : HOW LIBERAL AGEING, GROUP-COMPANY DEBTORS AND NBFC LAYERING CREATED A HIDDEN ₹1+ CRORE OVER-UTILISATION

1. Introduction

Samruddhi Bank Ltd., a mid-sized private sector bank, has been aggressively growing its MSME working capital portfolio. A new policy allows "banking-surrogate" working capital limits up to ₹2 crore where assessment can be largely based on KYC and bank statements, with limited reliance on audited financials and GST data.

In this backdrop, a branch proposes an enhancement-cum-takeover working capital limit for an existing borrower, based almost entirely on bank statements and collateral comfort. As the Credit Manager in the Regional Credit Hub, you are asked to examine whether the proposed structure is prudent or whether the file is a classic example of "turnover without real working capital discipline".

2. Borrower / Business Background

Borrower: Arjun Flexipack Industries Pvt. Ltd. (AFPL).

Constitution: Private Limited Company.

Promoters: i) Mr. Arjun Mehta - 48 years, B.Com, 20+ years in packaging trade. ii) Mrs. Neha Mehta - 45 years, homemaker, non-executive director.

Business Activity: AFPL manufactures printed flexible packaging material (laminated plastic rolls and pouches) for FMCG and agro-chemical companies in and around Gujarat.

Business Model & Working Capital Pattern (as per discussions with the borrower):

i) Raw material: Plastic granules and films purchased mostly on 30 - 45 days credit.

ii) Processing cycle: 20 - 25 days (printing, lamination, cutting, packing).

iii) Finished goods: Held for about 15 - 20 days before dispatch.

iv) Credit to buyers: Large FMCG clients insist on 60 - 90 days credit.

Thus, AFPL practically runs with: Total inventory period: approx. 40 - 45 days. Debtor days: 60 - 90 days. Creditor days: 30 - 45 days.

This inherently creates a working capital gap where cash goes out earlier (for raw material and operations) and comes back later (from debtors).

3. Existing Banking & Proposed Working Capital Facilities

Current Banking (with Jana Urban Bank Ltd.)

i) Cash Credit (Stock & Debtors): ₹3.00 crore.

ii) Term Loan - factory building: Outstanding ₹0.80 crore.

iii) Multiple unsecured business loans from NBFCs and fintechs: ₹0.60 crore (as visible in bank statements and CIBIL).

Account conduct is "formally standard" but with frequent overdrawals adjusted within 30 days, heavy routing of funds between group concerns, and EMI bouncing on NBFC loans (sometimes regularised within the same month).

Proposal to Samruddhi Bank

i) Takeover of Cash Credit limit of ₹3.00 crore.

ii) Enhancement of CC to ₹4.00 crore (Stock + Debtors).

iii) Fresh WCTL of ₹0.50 crore to consolidate high-cost NBFC loans.

iv) Collateral: a) Factory building at Bhuj GIDC - latest valuation ₹5.00 crore.
b) Residential flat of promoter - estimated value ₹1.20 crore.

Security cover appears strong at first look (overall security value approx. ₹6.20 crore against total requested exposure of ₹5.30 crore).

4. Key Developments

4.1 File Login and Available Information

Because this is proposed as a working capital "banking-surrogate" variant, the branch submits:

- Loan application and internal appraisal note.

- KYC of company and directors, ROC documents, PAN, Aadhaar, GST registration.
- Last 12 months' bank statements of AFPL's main current account with Jana Urban Bank (where CC operates).
- Last 6 months' stock statements submitted to existing bank.
- Property papers and valuation reports.

Audited financials for the latest year are "under finalisation"; the borrower is unwilling to share provisional financials, saying "everything is visible in banking". GST returns are partially shared for only 4 months, without any clear reconciliation with bank credits.

From a pure documentation checklist point of view, the file is incomplete for a normal working capital assessment - no full last 3 years' audited financials, incomplete GST, limited visibility on obligations of promoters, and no formal net worth statement. However, the branch insists that:

i) Turnover visible from bank statements is adequate for the requested limits.

ii) Collateral is strong and LTV is conservative.

iii) Relationship is "urgent" as the existing bank has started tightening DP and refusing adhoc limits.

You, as Credit Manager, decide to base your analysis on whatever is available, but with heightened caution as suggested for such limited-information cases.

4.2 Bank Statement Analysis

On detailed analysis of 12 months' bank statements of the main CC account you observe:

i) Annual credit summations (business-related credits) - around ₹28 crore.

ii) Last 4 months show a visible decline in monthly credits compared to the first 8 months.

iii) There are frequent transfers to and from sister concerns "Mehta Packaging" and "Mehta Traders", without clarity on underlying invoices.

iv) EMI debits of approx. ₹7 - 8 lakh per month towards various NBFC business loans and personal loans of promoters.

v) Multiple small ticket unsecured BL/BSL(Bilateral Loans/ Broadly Syndicated Loans) loans have been availed in the last 9 - 12 months.

vi) Occasional overdrawals above the CC limit, adjusted within 7 - 10 days by parking funds from sister concerns.

Given that you are relying heavily on banking, you treat credit summations from identified trade customers as proxy for sales, after removing own transfers, loan disbursals and capital infusions.

4.3 Stock Statements & Drawing Power

You also obtain the last 6 months' stock statements submitted by AFPL to the existing bank. Typical month shows (average figures):

- Raw Material + WIP + Finished Goods (Stock): ₹4.00 crore.
- Debtors: ₹5.00 crore.
- Creditors: ₹2.50 crore.

On that basis, existing bank has been calculating DP approximately as:

Stock + Debtors – Creditors = ₹4.00 + ₹5.00 - ₹2.50 = ₹6.50 crore.

Promoter's margin @ 25% = ₹1.63 crore.

Bank finance (gross DP) = (₹6.50 - ₹1.63) = ₹4.87 crore.

Against sanctioned CC of ₹3.00 crore and other WC facilities of around ₹1.25 crore (LC/BG/BD etc.), the CC account is almost fully utilised most of the time.

You decide to re-compute DP more conservatively using:

- Only stock within 180 days based on last 6 months' purchases.
- Only debtors up to 90 days (based on ageing shared during stock audit by existing bank).
- Exclusion of group-company debtors ("Mehta Packaging", "Mehta Traders").
- Full creditors, without age relaxation.

Revised eligibility (for one representative month) works out to roughly:

- Eligible Stock (≤180 days): ₹3.10 crore.

- Eligible Debtors (≤90 days, after excluding group and adjusting advances): ₹3.20 crore.
- Net Creditors (after adjusting advances to suppliers): ₹2.80 crore.

Net working capital requirement = ₹3.10 + ₹3.20 - ₹2.80 = ₹3.50 crore.

Promoter's margin @ 25% = approx. ₹0.88 crore.

Gross DP (total WC funding capacity) ≈ ₹2.62 crore.

Existing other WC facilities utilisation ≈ ₹0.80 crore.

Thus, actual CC Drawing Power ≈ ₹2.62 - ₹0.80 = ₹1.82 crore

Yet, the current CC outstanding at existing bank is hovering around ₹2.90 - 3.05 crore.

This means that, on a DP- correct basis, the account has been over-utilised by about ₹1.00 - 1.20 crore for a significant part of the year, temporarily masked by inflated stock statements and relaxed ageing norms.

4.4 Site Visit and Business Reality

During your factory visit, you observe:

a) Reasonable level of activity, but utilisation of machinery appears at ~ 60 - 65% of installed capacity.

b) Finished goods godown has slow-moving inventory of customised printed rolls for small regional brands which, according to staff, are stuck because clients are delaying payments.

c) On probing, you learn that some debtors are outstanding for more than 180 days and are repeatedly rolled over by adjusting invoices.

d) Promoter admits that margins are under pressure due to raw material price volatility and delayed payments from large FMCG clients.

The on-ground picture broadly confirms the banking trend - sales have flattened, collections are slowing, and the borrower is using short-term unsecured loans to plug working capital gaps.

4.5 Renewal Status and Short-Term Review at Existing Bank

From informal discussion with the existing bank's relationship manager, you come to know:

a) Annual renewal of WC limits is already overdue by around 4 months.

b) Bank has done only a 3-month short renewal earlier due to incomplete data and stress in business.

c) Current approach is to keep limits technically standard but tightly control DP and gradually reduce exposure.

d) Promoter is approaching Samruddhi Bank primarily to: Get enhanced CC limit, Regularise over-utilisation, and Refinance high-cost NBFC loans through WCTL.

This converts this case from a simple "growth" story into a potential stress migration case.

5. Problem Statement

a) Inflated stock statements and liberal debtor ageing at the existing bank are masking a genuine DP shortfall of about ₹1.0 - 1.2 crore in the current CC limit.

b) Annual credit summation (proxy sales) has started declining in the last 4 months, even as total bank and NBFC borrowings have increased, indicating possible over-leverage.

c) A significant portion of receivables is outstanding beyond 120 - 180 days and includes related-party/group debtors, raising concerns on the quality and realisability of current assets.

d) The proposal relies primarily on bank statements and partial GST data, without full audited financials, making it a high-risk banking-surrogate assessment at a relatively large ticket size.

e) Existing bank has already resorted to short-term renewal and DP-based control, suggesting emerging stress; the proposed enhancement at Samruddhi Bank may effectively be an "exit route" for the existing lender rather than genuine business growth.

f) Promoter is attempting to consolidate multiple unsecured NBFC loans into a WCTL, but continues to depend on external short-term borrowing for working capital gaps created by extended debtor days.

g) Though collateral cover appears strong, the core cash-flow-based working capital cycle is weak, raising the classic dilemma: "Should collateral comfort override clear red flags in DP and banking behaviour?"

6. Detailed Analysis

6.1 True Working Capital Requirement vs. Apparent Comfort

Conceptually, AFPL's working capital need arises because it must:

- Hold raw material and WIP for ~ 40 - 45 days.
- Provide 60 - 90 days credit to debtors.
- Receives only 30 - 45 days credit from suppliers.

This results in net funds being locked in stock and receivables for at least 60 - 90 days beyond supplier support, forcing the businessman to arrange extra working capital.

In theory, bank working capital limits should replace high-cost informal/short-term borrowing and stabilise the cycle. In AFPL's case, however, the opposite has happened:

- Formal CC limits have not been right-sized;
- Debtor discipline has weakened (stretching beyond 120 - 180 days);
- Promoter has layered NBFC loans on top of CC to plug recurring cash gaps.

This is a structural working capital stress, not a one-time temporary mismatch.

6.2 Limits Based Only on Bank Statements - What You See vs. What You Don't

When assessment is done purely on bank statements, the temptation is to say:

"Credit summation is ₹28 crore p.a., so sanctioning CC of ₹4 crore seems comfortable."

However, as banking-surrogate guidance clearly warns:

- Turnover alone does not reveal capital erosion, accumulated losses, or off-balance sheet liabilities.
- Heavy routing between related entities can artificially inflate credit summations.
- Declining monthly credits just before the borrower approaches a new bank is a serious red flag.

In this case:

- Last 4 months' credit summations are noticeably lower than the previous 8 months.
- EMI debits show aggressive NBFC borrowing in the recent past.
- Large related-party transfers are being routed through the same account.

A prudent credit professional cannot ignore these when most other documents (full financials, detailed GST reconciliation, ageing reports) are absent.

6.3 Drawing Power Discipline - The Real Control, Not the Sanction Limit

The revised DP computation (eligible stock + eligible debtors - creditors - promoter's margin - other WC facilities) brings true usable CC DP to ₹1.82 crore vs. current outstanding of approx. ₹3.0 crore.

This implies that:

- For months together, AFPL has effectively been operating on overdrawn funds, but under the garb of liberal DP at the existing bank.
- Any serious stock audit can trigger immediate reduction of DP, converting genuine business outstandings into "irregular" or "overdue" balances.

From a risk perspective, this means:

- AFPL is already beyond sustainable bank funding for its current asset base.
- Enhancement of CC to ₹4.0 crore would reward poor discipline and encourage further stretching of stock and debtors.

6.4 Short-Term Renewal and DP-Based Control - Signals from the Previous Lender

The existing bank's approach of granting only short-term renewal instead of full annual renewal, and placing stricter controls through DP discipline and clearly defined lending conditions, is a clear early warning signal. It indicates that:

- The lender is not fully comfortable with long-term continuance of exposure.

- The bank is using short-term review as a tool to pressurise the borrower to correct structural issues before granting full renewal.

For Samruddhi Bank, stepping in with a larger CC limit and a WCTL under these circumstances effectively means:

- Taking over an account where the risk is already recognised by the previous lender.
- Providing an exit route to them without sufficient comfort that underlying business fundamentals have improved.

6.5 Documentation Gaps and Compliance Risk

Standard working capital appraisal expects:

a) Last 3 years' audited financials and tax audit reports.

b) Full GST returns, reconciled with financials.

c) 12 months' bank statements from all main operative accounts.

d) Details of existing loans and security (including sanction letters and statements).

e) Stock statements, ageing analysis of debtors and creditors.

In this case, multiple elements are missing or partial. Processing an enhancement-cum-takeover purely on: partial GST data, incomplete financials, and 12 months of banking from only one account, would create serious post-facto defensibility issues if the account later slips into NPA.

6.6 Collateral Comfort vs. Cash Flow Reality

While collateral of ₹6.20 crore appears strong against proposed exposure of ₹5.30 crore, reliance solely on collateral for a working capital facility contradicts the basic principle that WC loans are meant to finance current assets and operating cycle, not to be long-term quasi-mortgage loans.

Moreover:

- If debtors are ageing beyond 180 days and stock includes slow-moving SKUs, liquidation of collateral in stress situations may still lead to haircuts and delays.
- Over-dependence on collateral often leads to complacency in monitoring current assets, DP, and cash flows.

7. Outcome / Final Decision

After detailed discussion with the promoter, branch, and risk team, Samruddhi Bank decides as follows:

a) No enhancement of working capital limit and no WCTL for consolidation of NBFC loans at present.

b) Offer a restricted CC facility of ₹2.00 crore only, structured as a fresh relationship (not a full takeover of existing ₹3.00 crore CC).

c) Make sanction conditional on:
   - Promoter bringing in fresh capital of ₹0.50 crore upfront.
   - Closure of at least ₹0.40 crore of high-cost NBFC loans from own sources (not from bank funds).
   - Execution of mortgage on factory building and residential flat with conservative internal LTV norms.

d) Apply strict DP norms:
   - Stock up to 180 days, debtors up to 90 days, exclusion of group debtors, full creditors.
   - Monthly stock statements and quarterly stock audits for first year.

e) Treat the first 6 months as a short-term review period, with clear focus on:
   - Reducing average debtor days below 100 days.
   - No fresh unsecured NBFC/fintech borrowing without prior bank approval.

The promoter does not agree to bring in fresh capital or to reduce NBFC borrowing materially, insisting on full take-over and enhancement as per original proposal. Given this rigid stance and the multiple red flags identified, Samruddhi Bank politely declines the proposal, recording in its credit note that:

"Despite adequate collateral, the working capital cycle, drawing power discipline and overall leverage profile do not meet the bank's risk appetite for a surrogate, largely banking-based assessment at this ticket size."

Within 9 months, market feedback (and later CIBIL) shows that AFPL's existing CC account at Jana Urban Bank has slipped into SMA-2 and is under close monitoring.

8. Key Lessons for Credit Professionals

a) Never let collateral comfort override a clearly weak working capital cycle and chronic DP shortfall - WC lending must remain cash-flow and current-asset driven.

b) In banking-surrogate products, treat bank statements as your "financial statements" and do the deepest possible analysis of credit summations, counterparties, trends and leverage before deciding.

c) Re-compute DP using strict ageing and exclusion of group debtors; if true DP is materially lower than outstanding, treat it as a big red flag and not a technicality.

d) Short-term renewal and DP-based control at the previous lender are not routine events – they are signals of underlying stress that a new bank must read very carefully.

e) Insist on minimum documentation hygiene (KYC, full financials, GST, stock statements, ageing) even in surrogate products; incomplete information should lead to tighter, not looser, risk appetite.

f) Always map the working capital cycle explicitly - stock days, debtor days, creditor days - and quantify the genuine gap the bank is expected to finance instead of blindly matching the borrower's requested limit.

g) When structure, data and conduct all point to emerging stress, the most professional decision is often a well-documented "decline with reasons", rather than a compromised sanction that later becomes indefensible in NPA and vigilance reviews.

Working Capital Loan Checklist

A. Basic Understanding & Initial Screening

1. Confirm that the requirement is genuine working capital (day-to-day business funding) and not for fixed assets, property purchase, or long-term purposes.
2. Understand the business model and operating cycle in simple terms – stock days, debtor days, and creditor days – and how these create the net working capital gap.
3. Identify the bankable working capital gap as:

Net WC requirement = stock + debtors – creditors, and ensure that this gap is what the bank finances.

4. Check whether the promoter has over-invested in fixed assets and under-invested in working capital; this is a classic SME mistake and a strong risk signal.
5. Ensure that the borrower is not already bridging WC gaps through distress measures like selling personal assets or large informal borrowings; plan to replace these with structured WC limits.

B. Documentation & KYC Hygiene

6. Ensure a properly filled, signed loan application form with photographs is the first document in the file; never process a file without a complete application.
7. Collect full entity KYC (GST registration, IEC for exporters, address proof) and tally name & address with the application form.
8. Collect individual KYC of promoters/partners/directors (PAN, Aadhaar, DL, Passport) and ensure OSV ("Original Seen & Verified") is marked on copies.
9. Ensure constitution documents are in place – Partnership Deed / COI, MOA, AOA, directors list, shareholding pattern / Trust Memorandum & Bye-Laws as applicable.
10. Collect promoter and guarantor obligation details – 6–12 months' loan statements for all existing loans (housing, auto, business, CC, property loans, unsecured loans) plus relevant sanction letters.
11. Collect last 3 years' audited financials (BS, P&L, Tax Audit Report, CARO, annexures) and verify CA signature, stamp, membership number, and UDIN through ICAI portal.
12. Obtain GST returns (monthly/quarterly) for current and unaudited years to validate turnover trends and reconcile with claimed sales.
13. Collect last 3 years' ITR + computation of income for all borrowers & guarantors to understand overall income profile and tax behaviour.
14. Take last 12 months' bank statements of all main operating accounts, ensuring clarity of name, account number, dates, entries and daily closing balances; get fresh copies if unreadable.

15. Obtain property papers and collateral documents, verify ownership, area, type of property, and ensure there is no undisclosed prior mortgage.
16. For existing CC borrowers, collect last 6 months' stock statements to evaluate DP discipline and stock movement.
17. Collect net worth statements, top 5 buyers/sellers, and a one-page business profile to complete 360° understanding of the borrower.

C. Working Capital Assessment & DP Discipline

18. Assess WC eligibility using appropriate MPBF norms (Naik Turnover Method, Tandon Method I/II) and remember that final limit is always the lower of (a) eligibility as per financial assessment, and (b) property / security coverage.
19. Ensure promoter's margin (typically 25%) is clearly brought into current assets; bank finance should not exceed about 75% of total WC requirement.
20. Calculate Drawing Power (DP) strictly from latest stock & debtors statements after deducting ineligible items (old debtors, advances, obsolete stock, etc. as per bank policy).
21. Remember that DP can never exceed the sanctioned limit; at any point, utilisation must be ≤ DP ≤ sanctioned CC limit.
22. Check that monthly DP calculation matches actual banking pattern – if credits are weak but DP is high, question the reliability of stock statements.

D. Banking-Surrogate / Limited-Information WC Cases

23. When working only with KYC + bank statement, strengthen KYC due diligence (CIBIL, address match, Google checks, segment risk, fraud alerts) and tighten risk appetite.
24. For such surrogate WC products, keep ticket size conservative (generally around ₹50 lakh–₹1 crore, subject to bank policy) and insist on high-quality collateral with tight LTV.
25. Perform deep bank statement analysis – treat genuine business credits from buyers as sales, excluding transfers, loans, capital entries, and unrelated credits.
26. Prepare month-wise credit summation and study trend (stable, growing, declining); declining credits just before proposal is a serious red flag and must be investigated.

27. Check if counterparties in banking match declared business; if the firm claims "garments trading" but credits are from unrelated segments, do not treat them as sales.
28. Examine concentration risk (few buyers/suppliers dominating flows) and related-party cross-flows that may artificially inflate turnover.
29. Make factory/business premises visit mandatory in such cases – physically verify activity level, stock, staffing, and promoter's understanding of business and WC cycle.
30. Do not sanction in surrogate cases if CIBIL is poor, business vintage is very low, or visit + banking picture does not give comfort, unless higher-level approvals and strong mitigants exist.

E. Renewal, Review & Commitments

31. For annual renewals, ensure updated financials, GST returns, bank statements, fresh CIBIL and EWS/RFA checks are obtained before extending limits.
32. Use short-term renewal or DP restriction (2–6 months) when you want commitments to be fulfilled (capital infusion, loan closure, leverage improvement) before allowing full-year DP.
33. If commitments are not met by the review date, be prepared to reduce DP to zero, treat the account as overdrawn/overdue, and initiate recall/SMA action as per policy.
34. For condition-compliance reviews (no new exposure), call only those specific documents which prove compliance (CA certificate for capital, GST/sales register for turnover, closure letters, etc.).
35. Always remember that working capital limits are payable on demand – use this legal position responsibly when risk is high and behaviour is not improving.

•••

CASE STUDY 14

FRUITS, FAKE TURNOVER AND 43B(H): WHY A "FULLY SECURED" FRUITS TRADER WORKING CAPITAL PROPOSAL WAS FLATLY REJECTED

1. Introduction

This case is based on a mid-sized private sector bank's credit hub reviewing a working capital proposal from a fruits trader.

Sales and business teams were confident it would be an easy sanction. The credit team, however, took a deeper view of the business model, cash flows, legal obligations, banking pattern and on-ground reality and finally rejected the file, despite security comfort. The case highlights that collateral cannot substitute cash-flow viability or promoter integrity.

2. Borrower & Business Background

Borrower: M/s FreshBloom Agro Traders.

Constitution: Partnership firm.

Promoter: Mr. Rohan Malhotra, 38 years.

Location: Nashik, Maharashtra.

FreshBloom is a nine-year-old wholesale fruits trading firm dealing in:

- Domestically sourced grapes, pomegranates, bananas and seasonal fruits.
- Imported apples and kiwis purchased through Mumbai-based importers.

The firm buys largely from:

- Local farmers' producer organisations (FPOs) and registered small traders (many classified as MSMEs).
- A few large importers for imported fruits.

It sells mainly to:

- Supermarkets and modern retail chains in Mumbai, Pune and Ahmedabad.
- Commission agents in APMC mandis in North India.

Financial performance as per CA-certified financials:

FY24: Sales - ₹14 crore; PAT - ₹18 lakh.

FY25: Sales - ₹18 crore; PAT - ₹24 lakh.

FY26: Sales - ₹17.5 crore; PAT - ₹22 lakh.

Margins of around 1.2 - 1.4% post-tax are in line with commodity-style fruits trading. Net worth as on FY26 is reported at around ₹2.20 crore. The business is classified as Standard - Fruits Trading in the bank's internal industry matrix, with moderate risk but highly seasonal cash flows.

3. Proposed Loan / Facility Structure

FreshBloom currently enjoys a cash credit limit of ₹1.80 crore with a cooperative bank in Nashik, secured by:

- Primary security: Hypothecation of stock and book debts.
- Collateral security: Equitable mortgage of a commercial godown property, latest valuation approx. ₹3.80 crore.

The promoter has approached a new bank with the following request:

i) Takeover of the existing ₹1.80 crore CC.

ii) Enhancement to a total ₹3.00 crore working capital (cash credit) limit.

Key representations by the promoter and sales team:

- Existing conduct is "satisfactory", no overdues.
- CIBIL score of main partner > 760.
- Business is "growing", with large supermarket orders in pipeline.
- Property provides > 200% collateral cover.

On this basis, the sales team pitched the deal as a "low-risk, collateral-backed takeover".

4. Scenario & Developments During Appraisal

4.1 Initial Financial Snapshot

Based on FY26 financials and CMA data submitted for the proposed year:

Turnover (FY26): ₹17.5 crore

Projected turnover (FY27): ₹22 crore

EBITDA margin: approx. 2.0%

PAT margin: approx. 1.25%

Reported current ratio: 1.10x

Total outside liabilities / Tangible net worth: 3.6x

4.2 Trigger for Deeper Scrutiny

The credit team noticed three aspects that did not sit well together:

i) Perishable stock with low reported stock days (12) - which is plausible for fruits,

ii) Very long debtor days (95) with large, powerful buyers (supermarkets), and

iii) Equally long creditor days (75) from MSME FPOs and small village traders - which was unusual and factually suspect given farmers' limited ability to give credit.

This contradiction, plus an aggressive enhancement request from ₹1.80 crore to ₹3.00 crore, prompted a deep dive into:

- Working capital calculations.
- Bank statements.
- On-site business activity.
- Legal obligations under MSME/Section 43B(h).

MSME Section 43B(h): As per the newly introduced clause (h), any amount payable by an assessee to a Micro or Small Enterprise that is paid after the time limit prescribed under Section 15 of the MSMED Act will be permitted as a tax deduction only in the financial year in which the payment is actually made, regardless of the accounting method followed.

In simple words, if dues to a Micro or Small Enterprise are cleared within 45 days, the expense can be claimed as a deduction in the same financial year. If the payment crosses the 45-day limit, the deduction will be available only in the year in which the payment is ultimately made.

5. Problem Statement

After the full appraisal, the bank crystallised five core issues:

a) Genuine working capital requirement was far lower than the requested limit, once the net working capital cycle was computed realistically rather than as projected.

b) Section 43B(h) obligations towards MSME suppliers made the business model structurally risky, given the much longer receivable cycle from large supermarket buyers.

c) Bank statement analysis revealed heavy concentration and possible round-tripping, with over 80% of credits and debits linked to a single large trading counterparty.

d) Site visit exposed a major mismatch between reported stock/activity and ground reality, calling into question both the scale of business and the quality/marketability of security.

e) Promoter behaviour and external conduct (overdue facilities, poor routing discipline, casual responses) undermined confidence in the borrower's intention and transparency, despite a superficially clean CIBIL and strong collateral.

6. Detailed Analysis

6.1 Working Capital Assessment & Product Suitability

Using the reported numbers, the projected net operating cycle is:

- Debtors: 95 days.
- Plus stock: 12 days.
- Less creditors: 75 days.
- Net cycle (as per CMA): 32 days.

On projected turnover of ₹22 crore, the working capital requirement becomes:

₹22 crore × 32 / 360 = ₹1.96 crore.

Assuming 25% margin from borrower and 75% bank finance, the fund-based requirement works out to roughly ₹1.45 crore. However, borrower already has ₹1.80 crore limit and is now requesting ₹3.00 crore which is almost double the genuine requirement.

This mirrors a common pattern seen in other rejected cases where limits far exceed working capital gaps, indicating that bank finance is being used as a quasi-term loan or for non-business purposes.

Additionally, as per internal policy aligned to RBI/Tandon norms, for limits beyond ₹1 crore, the bank prefers MPBF-based assessment and a minimum current ratio of 1.33x. FreshBloom's current ratio is only 1.10x, indicating stretched short-term liquidity and poor cushion for shocks.

The conclusion from this angle: The product (large CC limit) and quantum (₹3 crore) are not justified by the realistic working capital gap.

6.2 Legal & Regulatory Angle - MSME Suppliers and Section 43B(h)

On probing the purchase side, the credit manager discovered that:

i) Around 60 - 65% of purchases are from registered FPOs and small traders who qualify as MSMEs.

ii) In line with recent changes under Section 43B(h) of the Income-tax Act, payments to MSME suppliers are required to be made within 45 days for the expenditure to be allowed as a deduction.

However, FreshBloom's debtor cycle with large supermarket chains and big mandis was actually closer to 110 - 120 days (as seen from debtor ageing and collection pattern), not 95 days as shown in the CMA.

This creates a structural mismatch:

i) Outflows to MSME suppliers are legally constrained to 45 days,

ii) Inflows from powerful buyers come in 110 - 120 days,

iii) The gap cannot be bridged purely through margins and internal accruals.

In practical terms, this means: Either the borrower will default on MSME obligations, risking legal and reputational consequences, or he will stretch bank limits aggressively to fund this gap, turning the working capital account into a permanent, stressed source of MSME funding.

From a credit-risk standpoint, this is a time bomb - the business model itself is misaligned with legal obligations and cash-flow realities.

6.3 Bank Statement Scrutiny

The bank obtained 12 months' statements from both the existing CC account with the cooperative bank, and the borrower's main current account.

Key observations:

a) Over 82% of credits in the current account came from a single entity, Sai Om Distributors.

b) Around 79% of debits from the same account were also to Sai Om Distributors.

c) Multiple transactions were seen where:

   - ₹15 lakh came in from Sai Om in the morning, and
   - ₹15 lakh went out to Sai Om or related UPI IDs by evening,
   - On several days in a row, in neat round figures.

d) On cross-checking, Sai Om was found to be a partnership firm with common family links to the promoter's extended relatives.

This pattern is typical of round-tripping or accommodation entries i.e. artificially inflating credit turnover to show higher banking to justify higher limits and Window-dress turnover numbers, while actual physical stock movement may be limited.

Moreover, when the credit manager reconstructed unique trading flows (net of same-day in-and-out with the same party), the effective annual banking-linked turnover appeared closer to ₹8 - 9 crore, not the ₹17 - 18 crore shown in financials. This raised serious doubts about the genuineness of reported turnover, and the real working capital need.

6.4 Field Visit - Business Activity vs. Financial Claims

A unit visit was conducted to FreshBloom's primary godown and office in Nashik.

Findings:

a) The godown, reportedly holding ₹1.50 - 1.80 crore of stock on peak days as per CMA, actually had only a few stacks of crates, visually estimated at ₹25 - 30 lakh maximum.

b) No cold storage facility was functioning on site; rented cold storage used elsewhere was not adequately evidenced.

c) At 11:30 AM on a weekday, only two workers and one helper were present; no active loading/unloading, no transport vehicles, no billing activity.

d) The office was manned by a single accountant; the main partner arrived only after multiple calls from the relationship manager.

Regarding collateral:

a) The mortgaged godown property was in a semi-industrial belt with limited commercial demand.

b) Approach road was narrow, and several neighbouring units were either closed or converted to non-industrial use.

c) Market enquiries suggested that while valuation might be ₹3.80 crore on paper, actual realisable value in distress sale could be significantly lower.

In short, the on-ground business scale did not match the reported financials, and marketability of collateral in a default scenario was weaker than assumed.

6.5 Promoter Behaviour, External Conduct & Overall Risk View

Further checks revealed:

a) A small business loan from an NBFC had slipped into 30+ DPD in the past six months, though subsequently regularised.

b) A vehicle loan EMI had bounced multiple times in the last year.

c) The existing CC account with the cooperative bank had been in SMA-1 status twice in the last 12 months due to occasional overdrawals and delayed interest servicing.

When questioned about Round-tripping pattern with Sai Om Distributors, Limited stock on ground and Section 43B(h) implications, the promoter's responses were casual and evasive:

a) He claimed the large circular transactions were *"only temporary adjustments to help a friend's business"*.

b) He dismissed 43B(h) risk as *"only an income tax adjustment which CA will manage"*.

c) He insisted that business will *"definitely touch ₹25 crore next year"* without sharing concrete purchase orders or contracts.

This behaviour strongly resembled patterns seen in other cases where genuine business growth was absent, but borrowers sought to leverage collateral and manipulated banking figures to secure higher limits.

The internal risk rating, after factoring financials, conduct, business model risk, legal risk and behavioural risk, fell just short of the bank's minimum threshold for new working capital sanctions.

7. Outcome / Final Decision

After detailed discussion in the credit committee, the decision was to reject the proposal outright, with the following key points recorded on file:

a) Working capital gap does not justify the requested ₹3 crore CC limit, and even existing ₹1.80 crore appears high relative to realistic requirement.

b) Structural mismatch between MSME payment obligations (45 days under Section 43B(h)) and receivable cycle (110 - 120 days) makes the business inherently risky and prone to chronic over-utilisation and stress.

c) Bank statement forensics indicate possible round-tripping and inflated banking turnover, undermining trust in financial statements.

d) On-ground operations and stock levels are significantly lower than reported, raising questions on the genuineness of reported stock and sales.

e) Promoter behaviour and external conduct are not aligned with the bank's risk appetite, despite acceptable CIBIL and strong collateral.

The bank communicated a clear decline to the customer, without offering any reduced-quantum compromise, and made a note in internal systems to avoid future sanction to the same entity without substantial change in business model and transparency.

8. Key Lessons for Credit Professionals

a) Always compute the real working capital gap using realistic debtor, stock and creditor cycles; do not rely blindly on projections or turnover-based thumb rules.

b) Factor in legal obligations like Section 43B(h) for MSME suppliers - if cash inflows structurally lag mandatory outflows, the model is inherently high-risk, whatever the collateral.

c) Use bank statement forensics aggressively: look for concentration, same-party in-and-out entries and round-tripping patterns before believing reported turnover.

d) Never skip or dilute the unit visit - mismatch between physical stock/activity and book numbers is one of the strongest indicators of window-dressing or bogus billing.

e) Do not let collateral comfort override cash-flow viability and promoter integrity; a weak, manipulated business backed by strong property is still a bad credit.

f) Have the courage to say a clean "NO" even when everything looks fine on the surface (CIBIL, security, small limit, existing banking elsewhere); long-term portfolio quality depends more on deals you reject than on deals you book.

•••

CASE STUDY 15

PD MASTERCLASS: CONDUCTING A PERSONAL DISCUSSION FOR MSME WORKING CAPITAL - STEP-BY-STEP WITH SWEETCRUST BAKERS

This mock Personal Discussion (PD) has been designed to help credit professionals understand how a structured, purposeful PD should be conducted in a real lending scenario. Unlike a formal case study, this section focuses on the live interaction between borrower and banker on how to probe, interpret responses, identify red flags, and assess both business viability and borrower integrity. Through this bakery-shop example, credit officers will learn how to evaluate small MSME units, understand cash-intensive operations, analyse household and business linkages, and convert qualitative insights into concrete credit judgments.

PERSONAL DISCUSSION (PD) – SWEETCRUST BAKERS, LUCKNOW

Borrower: M/s SweetCrust Bakers - Proprietorship of Mr. Rohan Agarwal

Business: Retail bakery shop - cakes, pastries, breads, biscuits and snacks

Location: Ground-floor shop, Vishal Market, Aliganj, Lucknow

Purpose of PD: Fresh appraisal for working capital and small capex facility

Proposed Limit (overall): Around ₹15 - 20 lakh

1. Personal Background

Credit Manager (CM): Good morning, Mr. Agarwal. Please relax and treat this as a normal discussion. To start with, tell me a little about yourself and your family.

Borrower (B): Good morning, Sir. I am Rohan Agarwal, 32 years old, resident of Aliganj, Lucknow. I completed B.Com from a local college and then worked for about four years as a supervisor in a large bakery unit in Gomti Nagar. I am married, my wife is a homemaker and occasionally helps at the shop during rush hours. We have one daughter studying in Class 2. I stay with my parents in our own house at Aliganj.

CM: Who all are financially dependent on you?

B: My wife, daughter and partially my parents. My father receives a small pension from Railways, which covers some of their expenses, but I manage most of the household costs.

2. Business Background and Vintage

CM: When and how did you start SweetCrust Bakers?

B: I started this shop in October 2019. After working in the bakery industry, I wanted to start my own venture. One of my friends vacated this shop, so I took it on rent, invested around ₹8 lakh from my savings and family support for oven, display counters and initial stock, and started SweetCrust.

CM: Have you always run this single outlet?

B: Yes, only this outlet. I tried home delivery through food apps during COVID period, but it was through the same shop kitchen.

CM: How has the business trend been from the start till now?

B: First year was moderate as people got to know us. Then COVID lockdowns affected us; sales dropped sharply in 2020 - 21. After things normalised, sales picked up. Now in the last two years, business is stable and growing. We are known for customised birthday cakes in our locality.

3. Premises, Licences and Operations

CM: Is the shop owned or rented? What is the arrangement?

B: It is a rented shop of about 350 sq. ft. on ground floor. Current rent is ₹27,000 per month plus maintenance. I have a registered 3-year lease deed, renewed last year, valid up to September 2028.

CM: What licences do you maintain?

B: I have FSSAI licence in my firm's name, GST registration, Shop & Establishment certificate and Trade licence from Nagar Nigam. Fire safety norms are basic as my oven is electric, not gas based.

CM: How many staff work with you?

B: Four employees - one head baker, one helper in kitchen and two counter boys. They are on fixed salary, plus small incentive in festival seasons. I personally sit at the shop daily from 7 am to 10 pm.

4. Sales Profile, Customers, Seasonality

CM: Please explain your sales pattern like daily average, peak seasons, and customer profile.

B: On normal days, our sales are around ₹18,000 - ₹20,000 per day. On weekends and during festivals, it goes up to ₹30,000 - ₹35,000. Average monthly sales come around ₹5.5 - ₹6 lakh now. Customers are mainly walk-in retail customers from nearby colonies, plus some regular orders from coaching institutes and small offices for snacks and birthday celebrations. Peak seasons are wedding season, New Year, Christmas and school reopening times.

CM: What percentage is cakes and pastries versus biscuits and snacks?

B: Roughly 45% cakes and pastries, 35% breads and biscuits and 20% savoury snacks and beverages.

CM: How do customers usually pay - cash, UPI, cards?

B: Around 55 - 60% is cash, 35% UPI and remaining 5 - 10% through cards. For bigger party orders, many people pay via UPI or bank transfer.

5. Purchase, Suppliers and Stock Cycle

CM: Who are your main suppliers and what is your buying pattern?

B: I buy flour, sugar and basic ingredients from three wholesale dealers in Aminabad and Chowk. For cream, chocolate, decorations and premix, I buy from two specialised bakery suppliers based in Kanpur and Delhi. I usually purchase weekly. Credit period is 15 - 20 days for regular items and 7-10 days for speciality items.

CM: How much stock do you normally carry?

B: Raw material stock is about ₹3 - 4 lakh at cost - flour, sugar, premix, cream, packing material, etc. Finished goods inventory is low because bakery items have short shelf life. Cakes and pastries are produced daily; unsold items are discounted at end of day.

CM: Any single supplier on whom you are heavily dependent?

B: For premix and decorations, around 60% comes from one Kanpur supplier, BakeWorld Distributors. If needed, I can get similar items from other suppliers, but prices may be slightly higher.

6. Turnover, Margins and Book-keeping

CM: What was your turnover and profit in last three years?

B: Approximate figures are:

- FY 2023-24: Turnover around ₹42 lakh; net profit about ₹4.5 lakh.
- FY 2024-25: Turnover around ₹51 lakh; net profit about ₹5.8 lakh.
- FY 2025-26 (provisional): Turnover around ₹63 lakh; net profit roughly ₹7.2 lakh.

CM: Are these figures as per books or estimate?

B: These are as per my books and the data given to my CA. Some small cash sales may not be fully billed, but major sales, especially cakes and party orders, are billed and reported for GST.

CM: Who maintains your accounts and GST returns?

B: I maintain day-book and cash/UPI register myself. Once a month, I give data to my CA firm, M/s K & Associates, who prepare GST returns and final accounts.

CM: What is your gross margin?

B: On an average, gross margin is about 45% on cakes and 30 - 35% on biscuits and snacks. Overall blended gross margin is around 38 - 40%.

7. Banking Habits and Existing Borrowings

CM: Which banks do you currently operate with?

B: I have a current account in Shree Gramin Bank, Aliganj Branch, which I opened when I started the shop. Most UPI settlements and card settlements go there. I also have a savings account with Samrat Urban Co-operative Bank, where my old salary used to come.

CM: I noticed from your statements that monthly bank credits are around ₹3 - 3.5 lakh, whereas you mentioned sales of about ₹5.5 - ₹6 lakh. Why this difference?

B: Many small counter sales, especially biscuits and bread, are cash and used directly for petty expenses, purchase of milk and some raw material. I agree I should route more through bank; that is one reason I want to shift to a formal CC facility so I can regularise transactions.

CM: Do you have any existing loans?

B: Yes, a small business loan of ₹4.2 lakh from Shree Gramin Bank taken in 2025 under an MSME scheme. The EMI is ₹11,400 per month, running regularly. Additionally, I have an old personal loan of ₹1.8 lakh from Samrat Urban Co-operative Bank with EMI of ₹5,700, also regular. Apart from this, I have around ₹2.5 lakh informal hand loan from my uncle, used during COVID; I repay him ₹10,000 - ₹12,000 per month whenever surplus is available.

CM: Any credit card dues or other liabilities?

B: I have one credit card with limit of ₹75,000, used for online purchases of decorations. I clear it every month; no overdue.

8. Purpose and Requirement of Bank Finance

CM: Now tell me clearly what facility you are seeking from our bank and for what exact purpose.

B: I want a working capital facility because my cash is always tied up in stock and receivables from party orders. I also want to upgrade my oven and display counter. Therefore, I am seeking:

i) Cash Credit limit of around ₹10 lakh against stock and receivables.

ii) Term Loan of about ₹7 lakh for new electric deck oven and two refrigerated display counters.

CM: How will these additions help your business?

B: The new oven will increase capacity and improve quality, especially for bulk cake orders; currently my oven takes longer and power consumption is high. The better display counter will attract more walk-in customers. With CC limit, I will be able to get better credit terms from suppliers and stock more varieties, especially during festive seasons, leading to higher sales.

CM: How do you plan to repay the term loan?

B: I am comfortable with a 5-year tenure. Based on my projected increase in turnover to around ₹80 - 85 lakh in the next 2 - 3 years, I can service EMI of ₹16,000 - ₹18,000 per month.

9. Security, Margin and Own Contribution

CM: What security can you offer for the proposed limits?

B: For CC, I can offer hypothecation of stock and receivables. For the term loan, the primary security will be the bakery equipment. Additionally, my father is ready to give third-party guarantee and we can offer equitable mortgage on our residential house if required for comfort, though the house is already partly mortgaged for my sister's marriage loan with another bank; around ₹9 lakh is outstanding there.

CM: How much margin or own contribution will you bring for the new equipment?

B: Total cost is about ₹9 lakh; I can bring ₹2 lakh from my savings and supplier will give me some short-term credit. I seek a term loan of ₹7 lakh from the bank.

10. Household Expenses, Insurance and Contingencies

CM: What is your average monthly household expenditure?

B: Around ₹40,000 including school fees, groceries, utilities and medical. After meeting business expenses and EMIs, I keep household expenses within this limit.

CM: Do you have life or medical insurance?

B: I have one term insurance policy of ₹50 lakh and a family health insurance cover of ₹5 lakh, both with regular premiums.

CM: Any major upcoming commitments like children's education, marriage, property purchase, etc.?

B: No major commitments in next 3 - 4 years except regular school fee and occasional family functions.

11. Guarantor's Interaction (Father)

CM: Namaste, Mr. Agarwal (Senior). Please share your background and your comfort with becoming guarantor.

Guarantor (G): Namaste, Sir. I am Mahesh Agarwal, 62, retired Section Officer from Indian Railways. I receive pension of about ₹38,000 per month. We live in our own house in Aliganj, in my name and my wife's name jointly. I have two children; my daughter is married and settled in Kanpur, and Rohan is younger, running this bakery.

CM: Are there any loans in your name?

G: Yes, there is a mortgage loan of about ₹9 lakh from Samrat Urban Co-operative Bank taken three years ago for my daughter's marriage. EMI is ₹19,000, which I pay from my pension. There is no default. Other than this, no borrowings.

CM: Are you aware of the details of Rohan's business and this proposed loan?

G: Yes, he discusses everything with me. I sit in the shop in the mornings sometimes. I know his sales pattern and that he has potential to expand. I am comfortable standing as guarantor because I have seen him managing the business responsibly, even during COVID.

CM: In case of any difficulty in repayment, how will you support?

G: To the extent of my pension and savings, I will support. If required, we can even liquidate some of my fixed deposits.

12. Closing Questions and Borrower's Attitude

CM: Is there any other information relevant for our credit assessment that you wish to share?

B: Only that I want to shift my main current account to your bank if my facilities are sanctioned. I will route all UPI and card settlements through your bank and close the old current account gradually. I am also willing to implement better billing and accounting practices as your bank suggests.

CM: If business slows down due to competition or any external factor, how will you manage?

B: I will cut down non-essential expenses, renegotiate with suppliers, and focus on high-margin products like customised cakes. I am ready to work longer hours and even start small catering for schools and offices to diversify income.

CM: Thank you, Mr. Agarwal. Your answers have been clear and straightforward. We will analyse the financials, verify documents and then revert.

B: Thank you, Sir.

Credit Manager's Detailed Observations and Analysis

The Credit Manager made the following observation:

The borrower, M/s SweetCrust Bakers (Proprietor: Mr. Rohan Agarwal), operates a single-outlet bakery in a good residential catchment of Aliganj, Lucknow. Business vintage is about 7.5 years, backed by prior employment experience in the same line. Location, visibility and footfall appear favourable for a small retail food unit. Product mix (cakes, pastries, breads and snacks) and strong demand for customised birthday cakes provide some niche positioning and repeat clientele. Overall, the Credit Manager views the business model as simple, understandable and within the bank's risk appetite for small MSME retail.

From the PD and declared figures, turnover has grown from around ₹42 lakh to ₹63 lakh over three years, with reported net profit improving from ₹4.5 lakh to about ₹7.2 lakh. Gross margins in the 38 - 40% range are consistent with bakery trade. While the books are prepared by a CA and GST is regularly filed, the borrower has admitted that some small cash sales are not billed and are used directly for expenses. The Credit Manager has therefore noted that actual business volume is likely higher than reported, but banking turnover is lower than the true scale, which is a risk from monitoring as well as income-tax/GST perspective. Nevertheless, the trend in profitability and the ability to meet existing EMIs without delay indicate reasonable repayment capacity.

Bank statements show average monthly credits of about ₹3 - 3.5 lakh against self-reported sales of ₹5.5 - ₹6 lakh. This gap reinforces the cash-routing issue. However, no cheque returns or adverse remarks are seen, and EMIs for existing loans of ₹4.2 lakh (business loan) and ₹1.8 lakh (personal loan) are regular. There is also an informal family borrowing of around ₹2.5 lakh, which the borrower is repaying gradually. The Credit Manager has recorded that total fixed obligations (including proposed term loan EMI) should be carefully computed and stress-tested against conservative cash accruals, but current FOIR appears manageable if projected sales materialise and if routing of transactions improves.

On the qualitative side, the borrower came across as straightforward, transparent and reasonably knowledgeable about cost structures, margins and seasonality. He could clearly explain his peak seasons, daily sales pattern, major cost heads and supplier terms, which reflects close involvement in day-to-day operations. The guarantor, a retired Railways employee with steady pension, is fully aware of the business and the proposed facilities, and has expressed willingness to support in contingencies. This provides an additional comfort on integrity and support system, though the guarantor's house is already partly mortgaged elsewhere.

In terms of risks, the Credit Manager has identified:

a) **Cash-intensive operations and low routing through bank,** which weakens cash-flow visibility and may affect assessment of turnover for future enhancements.

b) **Dependence on one major supplier for speciality materials,** creating some supply-chain risk and potential margin pressure.

c) **Existing informal borrowing from relative,** though this is interest-light and being serviced.

d) **Short shelf life of inventory,** which requires tight monitoring of stock quality and levels, especially if CC limit is sanctioned against stock.

As mitigants, the Credit Manager proposes that:

a) The sanction should be structured with clear stipulation to route minimum 75–80% of sales through the bank, with periodic review of bank turnover vis-à-vis GST/financials.

b) GST returns, IT returns and stock statements should be obtained and monitored regularly.

c) CC limit may be kept at a moderate level (around ₹10 lakh) linked to verified stock and receivables, and term loan of about ₹7 lakh may be structured with 5-year tenure, ensuring satisfactory DSCR based on conservative projections.

d) Primary security (stock, receivables and equipment) along with personal guarantee of the proprietor and third-party guarantee of the father should be obtained. Additional mortgage comfort can be considered at a later stage if required and legally feasible.

Overall, based on PD findings, business conduct and initial financial trend, the Credit Manager's analysis is that the proposal appears prima facie bankable as a small MSME working capital and capex case, provided the above conditions and monitoring requirements are imposed and complied with. Final decision would be subject to satisfactory verification of financials, CIBIL reports, site visit, valuation and verification of securities, and adherence to internal credit policy and RBI norms on MSME lending.

PD Checklist for Credit Managers:

1. Always begin the PD by making the borrower comfortable and encouraging open, honest communication.
2. Ask open-ended questions to understand the borrower's motivation, vision and involvement in the business.
3. Verify backward and forward linkages to gauge the borrower's understanding of supply chain and market reach.
4. Observe the borrower's confidence, clarity and consistency while responding to business and financial questions.
5. Check truthfulness by asking the same information in different ways during the conversation.
6. Assess social, financial and credit background based on borrower's behaviour, language and attitude.
7. Avoid leading questions and let the borrower narrate their business model freely.

8. Ensure the discussion covers business history, future plans, competition, and sustainability of the venture.
9. Note down all critical points of discussion and reconfirm them with the borrower during the PD.
10. Probe into the source of margin money, household expenses, and non-business financial obligations.
11. Ask questions about machinery, licenses, location, and asset ownership to validate business stability.
12. Evaluate borrower's knowledge about sales, margins, stock levels, supplier terms and customer profile.
13. Cross-check declared turnover with banking habits, GST filings, and purchase patterns.
14. Understand family background, involvement of relatives, and support systems available to the borrower.
15. Explore past financial discipline, EMI behaviour, and informal borrowings or liabilities.
16. Probe into future expansion plans and the borrower's logic behind the requirement of bank finance.
17. Discuss guarantor's awareness, willingness and financial strength during a separate interaction.
18. Compare PD inputs with documents later to detect inconsistencies or signs of misrepresentation.
19. Conduct at least one indirect question to judge whether the borrower tends to hide adverse facts or willingly discloses them.
20. Assess the borrower's ability to handle adversity by asking scenario-based "What if..." questions related to sales decline, supplier issues or personal emergencies.

•••

CASE STUDY 16

FROM ₹8 LAKH TO ₹5 LAKH: THE ART OF RIGHT-SIZING LIMITS IN INFORMAL BUSINESSES: USING PD INSIGHTS TO CALIBRATE EXPOSURE, BUILD IN SAFEGUARDS AND STILL SUPPORT A GENUINE SMALL ENTREPRENEUR

1. Introduction

A small kirana* shop in Raipur, Chhattisgarh approaches a commercial bank for a working capital facility.

*(*kirana – Local word for Grocery Shop)*

However, when the credit officer conducts a detailed Personal Discussion (PD) at the shop and combines it with external checks, the story changes. The PD reveals inconsistencies in turnover, margin exaggeration, structural weaknesses linked to the rented premises, and cash-flows routed through a different family member's account.

This case shows how granular questioning, on-site observation and simple cross-verification can completely alter the risk perception and final sanction terms.

2. Borrower & Business Background

Borrower: Mr. Rakesh Verma, 38 years, proprietor of "Annapurna General Store" located in a residential locality of Raipur, Chhattisgarh.

Business Profile:

- Nature: Retail kirana shop selling groceries and FMCG products.
- Location: Ground-floor shop in a mixed residential–commercial lane in Raipur.
- Vintage: 2.5 years in current shop. Before this, Rakesh worked for 5 years as a sales assistant in another kirana shop in Raipur.

- Ownership: First-generation entrepreneur; the shop is not an inherited family business.
- Premises: Rented shop on the ground floor of an old building; moderate frontage, steady local footfall.
- Product Range: Food grains, pulses, edible oil, sugar, packaged food, biscuits, tea/coffee, soaps, detergents, soft drinks and ice-cream.

Stated Financials (as per loan application & branch note):

a) Declared average monthly sales: ₹3.00 lakh.

b) Declared net monthly profit (after expenses): ₹60,000 - ₹70,000.

c) Other income: Nil (spouse is homemaker, no separate business).

d) Banking relationship:

One savings account (3+ years).

One current account (1+ year).

No cheque returns or adverse remarks reported.

3. Type of Loan / Facility Details

The branch proposes a working capital facility to support inventory and customer credit:

- Facility Type: Cash Credit (hypothecation of stock & book debts).
- Proposed Limit: ₹8.00 lakh.
- Primary Security: Hypothecation of stocks and sundry debtors of the shop.
- Collateral Security: Not insisted (small-ticket MSME, within policy dispensations).
- Tenor: Ongoing CC with annual review.
- Interest: MCLR-linked rate as per internal risk-grade based pricing.
- Repayment: On-demand facility; interest to be serviced monthly, with turnover requirement as per sanction terms.

Given that there is no immovable collateral and the facility is primarily secured by stock and book debts, the quality of PD and cash-flow assessment becomes critical.

4. Key Developments

The credit officer, Ms. Nandita Rao, visits Annapurna General Store in the early evening, a peak time in summer when households typically buy groceries and cold drinks. She uses a structured PD checklist of about 20 key questions covering: business vintage, nature of premises, product mix, sourcing pattern, supplier credit, daily sales, customer credit, stock management, expired goods handling, staff costs, cash-flow discipline, and shop timings.

At first glance, the shop appears busy and active, with a decent flow of customers. Shelves are reasonably stocked, and a single-door fridge displays soft drinks and ice-cream.

As Nandita progresses with the PD, she notices multiple points where numbers, behaviour and ground reality do not fully align with the declarations in the file.

5. Problem Statement

a) Declared turnover and profit margins appear overstated when reconciled with PD responses, stock levels and supplier purchase documents.

b) The business operates from rented premises with informal tenancy terms, creating material continuity and displacement risk.

c) High dependence on informal credit, both from suppliers and to customers, makes the working capital cycle volatile and weakens receivable quality.

d) A mismatch between the QR code beneficiary and the loan applicant's operative account raises KYC and cash-flow control concerns.

6. Detailed Analysis

6.1 Business Vintage, Experience and Reputation

Rakesh states that Annapurna General Store has been running in its present form for 2.5 years. He earlier worked for 5 years in another kirana shop in Raipur as a salaried employee, where he learned procurement, pricing and dealing with local customers.

From a credit standpoint, total experience in kirana trade exceeds the typical informal benchmark of 3 years. EPC (Enquiries with Persons Concerned) with neighbouring shops confirms that the present store has been functioning "for 2 - 3 years" and that Rakesh is generally soft-spoken and reliable. No major adverse remark or negative conduct is reported.

However, the standalone business vintage of 2.5 years is still relatively short. In a competitive kirana market, this leaves the business vulnerable to rent hikes, new entrants and local disruptions.

6.2 Premises: Rented Shop and Tenancy Risk

The shop is on rent. PD reveals the following details:

- Rent: ₹12,000 per month
- Agreement: Simple 11-month agreement, renewed once; currently about 6 months remain in the ongoing term
- Registration: Unregistered; mostly on mutual understanding

This has two implications:

a) **Fixed Cost Impact:** Rent must be treated as a fixed operating expense while estimating net profit. Overlooking this can artificially inflate net income and DSCR.

b) **Continuity / Displacement Risk:** In kirana trade, the location i.e. visibility, accessibility and "habit" of customers is the real asset. If the landlord raises rent sharply or refuses renewal, Rakesh may be forced to vacate. A shift to a smaller or less visible lane can cause an immediate drop in turnover, which would directly affect CC servicing.

For a working capital facility without collateral, this tenancy risk is significant and must be recognised in risk grading and limit sizing.

6.3 Turnover and Margin Realism

When asked about daily sales, Rakesh initially states:

"Daily sale is around ₹8,000 - ₹10,000."

On further probing, and when asked to describe different days, he mentions:

"Some days ₹5,000, some days ₹7,000, on Sundays maybe ₹12,000."

Nandita cross-checks these claims against:

a) Physical stock on shelves and in the small rear storage.

b) Purchase invoices from wholesalers and distributors for the last 2 - 3 months.

c) Space constraints and depth of product range.

Based on this triangulation, she estimates a realistic average daily sale in the range of ₹6,000 - ₹7,000, translating to monthly sales of about ₹1.8 - ₹2.1 lakh, not ₹3.00 lakh as declared.

On margins, Rakesh claims:

"On ₹10,000 sale, I save around ₹3,500."

This implies 35% net margin, which is unusually high for this segment. In kirana trade, gross margins are usually around 15 - 20%, with net margins after expenses generally within 8 - 12% for small shops.

The margin claim is therefore considered exaggerated. For credit assessment, the officer normalises net income to a conservative level based on realistic sales and typical trade margins.

6.4 Sourcing, Supplier Credit and Customer Credit

Rakesh purchases from two main wholesalers and some authorised distributors in Raipur. Credit terms:

a) Wholesalers: Average credit 15 - 20 days for staples and high-volume items

b) Distributors: Usually 7 - 10 days

He, however, extends credit to about 25 - 30 regular households in the surrounding area. Their monthly bills range from ₹3,000 - ₹5,000 each, and payments are collected typically every 30 - 45 days.

As per PD:

a) Outstanding receivables in the market at any time: roughly ₹1.0 - ₹1.2 lakh.

b) No formal ledger or software; customer credit is tracked in notebooks and diaries.

This creates a structural mismatch:

- Stock is purchased partly on 15 - 20 day credit.
- But cash is realised from customers after 30 - 45 days.

The longer receivable period w.r.t. creditor days stretches liquidity and makes Rakesh dependent on rolling supplier credit, informal borrowings or delayed payments.

For a CC based on stock and book debts, these receivables are not fully documented or legally enforceable in a standard way. This reduces effective security value and increases the risk of over-financing.

6.5 Inventory Management and Expired Goods

On enquiry about expired and slow-moving goods, Rakesh admits:

a) Some expired biscuits and packaged snacks accumulate occasionally.

b) He tries to sell near-expiry goods at discounts.

c) Small quantities are simply written off informally.

There is no systematic tracking of expiry dates, no defined process for return to supplier and no formal accounting for write-offs.

Implications:

a) Valuation of stock declared to the bank may be higher than its realistic marketable value

b) Losses from expired goods are hidden within "miscellaneous" expenses or not recorded at all

c) Security cover in a CC facility could be weaker than reported due to dead stock and obsolete items

6.6 QR Code, Cash-Flows and KYC Consistency

A key finding emerges when Nandita scans the QR code displayed at the counter:

a) QR beneficiary name: "Anita Verma", the borrower's spouse.

b) Loan and current account: In the name of "Rakesh Verma - Annapurna General Store (Proprietor)".

c) Shop signboard: "Annapurna General Store - Prop. R. Verma".

Rakesh explains that initially, he did not have a current account, so he linked the QR to his wife's savings account. He now has a current account in his own name, but has not updated the QR arrangement

Though this may not be fraudulent, it creates cash-flow leakage and control risk:

a) Digital receipts from customers are routed to an account not in the borrower's business name.

b) Tracing actual turnover through the current account becomes difficult.

c) Monitoring end-use and turnover compliance becomes less effective.

Given KYC and AML expectations and the need to assess genuine business flows, such a mismatch must be corrected as a pre-condition before allowing significant working capital limits.

6.7 Staff, Fixed Expenses and Repayment Capacity

Staff & fixed expenses (as per PD):

Helper salary: ₹7,000 per month.

Shop rent: ₹12,000 per month.

Electricity: Approx. ₹3,000 per month.

Miscellaneous overheads: Approx. ₹2,000 per month.

Total fixed expenses: about ₹24,000 per month (excluding family drawings).

Assuming realistic net monthly income of around ₹30,000 - ₹35,000 (instead of the declared ₹60,000 - ₹70,000), headroom for servicing interest on an ₹8.00 lakh CC is limited. Any temporary dip in sales or delay in customer collections could quickly strain cash-flows.

7. Outcome / Final Decision

After reviewing the PD findings, EPC feedback and the initial proposal, the credit manager draws the following conclusions:

a) The borrower is genuine, has basic experience in kirana trade, and runs a functioning shop with regular customers in Raipur.

b) However, turnover and net margin are significantly overstated in the application.

c) Rented premises with short-term tenancy, high customer credit, inadequate documentation of receivables, and QR code mismatch together create a higher risk profile than initially perceived.

Granting the full proposed CC limit of ₹8.00 lakh could result in:

- Underutilization of limit due to lower actual working capital requirement.
- Increased temptation to use surplus funds for non-business purposes.
- Higher probability of stress if any adverse shock hits the business.

Final Sanction Decision

a) **Downsizing and Restructuring of Facility**

  - Sanctioned facility: Cash Credit limit of ₹5.00 lakh instead of ₹8.00 lakh.
  - Security: Hypothecation of stock and sundry debtors, with drawing power linked to verified stock and book debts.
  - Turnover Requirement: Adequate annual turnover through the current account to be monitored; persistent non-compliance to trigger review.

b) **QR Code and Cash-Flow Alignment - Pre-disbursement Condition**

  Before activation of the CC limit, Rakesh must:

- Shift the primary business QR code to the current account in the name of "Rakesh Verma – Annapurna General Store".
- Submit evidence (screenshot / confirmation from payment app) to the branch.

c) **Monitoring & PD Conditions**

  - At least one structured PD every year and one surprise visit during the review cycle.
  - During visits, the officer to confirm: a) Business is operating from the same premises in Raipur.

b) Stock level and customer footfall are broadly consistent with reported turnover.

c) No major, undisclosed changes in business pattern.

d) **Advisory on Record-Keeping**

  - Rakesh is advised to maintain a simple daily sales register and a customer credit ledger (in notebook or basic mobile app).

- Over time, he is encouraged to route majority of business receipts and payments through the current account to establish a strong banking profile and facilitate future enhancements.

The bank thus supports a genuine small entrepreneur in Raipur with a calibrated exposure while protecting its asset quality and adhering to prudential norms.

8. Key Lessons for Credit Professionals

a) Use PD to rebuild the financials from ground reality - cross-check declared turnover and profit with stock levels, invoices, footfall and simple probing questions.

b) Treat tenancy and location as core risk factors in kirana finance - short, informal rent agreements can undo an otherwise stable business if displacement occurs.

c) Look beyond stock to the quality of receivables - unrecorded customer credit and long collection cycles can seriously weaken working capital and security value.

d) Always align cash flows with the borrower's operative account. Any mismatch between the QR code and the account name must be rectified to ensure accurate KYC compliance, effective monitoring, and proper adherence to loan terms and conditions.

e) Right-size limits for informal MSME borrowers - avoid over-financing; calibrate exposure to realistic cash-flows and insist on simple but disciplined record-keeping and periodic PD.

•••

CASE STUDY 17

HIGHWAY DHABA, HIGH FOIR: A SEMI-URBAN LAP CASE WHERE CIBIL, KCC AND CASH INCOME COLLIDE

1. Introduction

This case is set in Sadhuwali, a small town near Sri Ganganagar in Rajasthan. It focuses on a Loan Against Property (LAP) proposal from a self-employed, non-professional (SE-NP) borrower who runs a highway dhaba.

The borrower had long business vintage, self-owned residential property, and reasonably healthy bureau scores. Underneath, however, lie FOIR stress, bureau anomalies on KCC loans, mixed end-use, and a fully cash-driven business model. The case shows how disciplined PD(Personal Discussion), eligibility working, and controlled policy deviation can convert a borderline request into a defendable sanction.

2. Borrower & Business Background

Applicant: Mr. Lokesh Choudhary, 45 years.

Co-applicant: Mrs. Anita Choudhary, 40 years.

Lokesh lives with his parents, wife and college-going son in a self-owned, single-storey house in Sadhuwali. His father manages a small piece of agricultural land on the outskirts of the town; other family members are homemakers or students. Household expenses, children's education and most family obligations are met from the dhaba income.

For the last 10 - 11 years, Lokesh has been running M/s Nirmal Highway Dhaba & Family Garden on the Sadhuwali-Sri Ganganagar highway. The dhaba serves typical Punjabi-Rajasthani highway food.

Key business features recorded during PD:

a) Six staff members on fixed monthly salaries; combined wage bill ₹30,000 per month.

b) Premises are rented; monthly rent ₹10,000.

c) Average daily footfall 40-50, with average spend per customer ₹150-₹200.

d) Estimated monthly turnover in the range of ₹2.20-₹2.60 lakh.

Lokesh states that, after all expenses, he retains about ₹50,000-₹60,000 per month as profit. Instead of accepting this at face value, the credit officer decides to construct income scientifically using a dish-wise, PD-based working.

3. Collateral & Existing Banking Exposure

Lokesh offers his self-owned residential house in Sadhuwali as security. The property is in a largely developed colony (habitation around 80%) with good road access. The bank's panel valuer estimates a market value of ₹45 lakh. Title search shows clear and marketable title with no existing charge.

Key facilities appearing in CIBIL:

Auto Loan - Desert City Finance Bank

- Sanctioned amount: approx. ₹11.70 lakh
- Current balance: about ₹1.50 lakh
- EMI: ₹15,750, residual tenor 11 months

Kisan Credit Card (KCC) - Krishi Pragati Bank (Lokesh)

- Limit: ₹3.00 lakh, secured against ancestral agricultural land; account reported as standard.

Old KCC - Krishi Pragati Bank (Lokesh)

- Limit: ₹2.10 lakh
- CIBIL shows overdue of around ₹69,000.

KCC - Nirmal Cooperative Bank (Anita)

- Limit: ₹2.20 lakh, small running balance.

CIBIL scores are:

- Lokesh: 730.
- Anita: 626, largely due to imperfect reporting of KCC renewals.

These scores are acceptable but require deeper analysis, especially given the overdue appearing in Lokesh's old KCC.

4. Facility & End-Use

Lokesh has applied to Thar Gramin Bank for a LAP of ₹25 lakh against his house. Proposed facility structure:

Product: Loan Against Property - Term Loan

Amount requested: ₹25,00,000

Tenor: 180 months (15 years)

Indicative ROI: 12% p.a. (floating)

Security: Equitable mortgage of residential property + personal guarantees of both applicants.

End-use declared:

a) Business expansion: building covered seating, improving kitchen and storage, adding better sanitation facilities and signage to attract family travellers - estimated utilisation ₹15-16 lakh.

b) Debt consolidation: repaying multiple high-cost informal borrowings and some smaller loans within the family/social circle from the balance amount.

Bank's LAP policy caps LTV at 65% and FOIR at 60%, with power to allow FOIR deviation up to 5% (i.e., up to 65%) at higher sanctioning levels.

5. Current Scenario & Developments

During PD, the credit officer spends time at the dhaba across both afternoon and evening peaks. Based on observation and discussion, a simplified dish-wise income working is prepared:

Average daily revenue from various dish orders aggregates to around ₹7,500-₹8,000 per day.

Instead of multiplying by 30, the officer uses 25 working days to factor weekly lows, off-days and lean periods – a conservative and widely accepted practice in underwriting SE-NP cash businesses. This yields estimated monthly turnover of about ₹2.30-₹2.40 lakh, matching the broad band indicated by the customer.

From this, expense assumptions:

a) Raw material cost 50% of sales (vegetables, flour, spices, chicken, oil etc.).

b) Rent ₹10,000, staff salaries ₹30,000, and other overheads (gas cylinders, electricity, cleaning, minor repairs) about ₹10,000 per month.

After deducting all, the net monthly income is prudently assessed at around ₹40,000-₹41,000. For eligibility, the bank freezes ₹40,200 as the working figure, lower than the customer's claimed ₹50-60k, but more consistent with PD observations.

6. Problem Statement

a) **FOIR breach at the requested amount:** At ₹25 lakh, the projected EMI pushes FOIR well beyond the 60% policy cap and even higher than the 65% deviation ceiling.

b) **Co-applicant's modest CIBIL score (626):** The low score is driven by KCC reporting issues, but on the surface it raises doubts regarding repayment discipline.

c) **Overdue in Lokesh's old KCC:** CIBIL shows an outstanding overdue of about ₹69,000, creating potential conflict with RBI's IRAC norms and questioning the borrower's credit culture.

d) **Mixed end-use (expansion + consolidation):** Part of the LAP is for productive use, while part is for debt consolidation, which can mask over-leveraging and makes end-use monitoring more complex.

e) **Fully cash-based dhaba with limited formal financials:** Income estimation depends heavily on PD and judgement; any over-optimism directly distorts FOIR.

f) **Semi-urban collateral located approx. 25 km from branch**: Though LTV is low, realisation in stress may be slower than in a metro, requiring stronger structural safeguards.

7. Detailed Analysis

7.1 Eligibility, FOIR and LTV

Using the bank's LAP grid:

- ₹25 lakh at 12% for 180 months gives an EMI of roughly ₹30,000.
- With net income of ₹40,200, FOIR works out to around 74-75%, far exceeding even the deviation limit.

The officer therefore performs a back-solved eligibility calculation. By reducing the notional loan amount and re-running the FOIR, the following emerges:

a) At ₹21-21.5 lakh, EMI falls near ₹25,000-₹25,500 and FOIR moderates to around 63-64%, which, while above policy FOIR of 60%, remains within the 65% deviation band.

b) On the same property value of ₹45 lakh, LTV at ₹21.5 lakh is about 48% - very comfortable.

Thus, the internally supportable amount based purely on FOIR is in the ₹21-22 lakh range, not ₹25 lakh. LTV is not the constraint; income is.

7.2 Treatment of Existing Obligations

Bank's retail policy provides:

a) EMIs for loans with remaining tenor less than 12 months may be ignored for FOIR, subject to clean repayment track.

b) Agricultural KCCs against agricultural land without fixed EMIs can be treated as non-obligated for FOIR in retail LAP, provided the accounts are standard.

Accordingly, the auto loan (11 months left) is treated as non-obligated, with a remark in CAM (Customer Appraisal Memo) citing residual tenor and repayment track. Lokesh's current KCC and Anita's KCC are recorded but not loaded as EMIs in FOIR; instead, they are analysed qualitatively under "Other Borrowings".

This is aligned with usual banking practice and does not conflict with RBI guidelines, as FOIR is an internal risk metric and does not change classification under IRAC.

7.3 CIBIL, KCC Overdues and Regulatory Perspective

Two separate issues are addressed:

a) **Anita's CIBIL 626:**

On enquiry with Nirmal Cooperative Bank, the KCC in Anita's name is found to be regularly renewed each year. The CIC(Credit Information Company) file has not captured certain renewal events, depressing the bureau score. SOA(Statement of Accounts) shows no past-due beyond 30 days. The credit note documents this mismatch and attaches SOA, concluding that the low score is technical rather than behavioural.

b) **Lokesh's old KCC overdue (around ₹69,000):**

Here, bureau data indicates arrears. Even if Krishi Pragati Bank calls the account "standard", regularisation and overdue clearance are necessary to avoid backdoor evergreening and to respect RBI's IRAC norms on overdue recognition.

Sanction is therefore proposed with a non-negotiable pre-disbursement condition: Lokesh must clear the entire ₹69,000 overdue and provide updated SOA and a no-overdue/closure letter before the LAP disbursement. This condition converts a potential structural weakness into a risk mitigant; the LAP proceeds indirectly help in cleaning up the agricultural exposure, but only after proof of clearance.

7.4 End-Use Control and Monitoring

RBI's guidance on end-use of funds expects banks to ensure that term-loan funds are used for sanctioned purposes and not diverted to speculative or unrelated activities. In this case, mixed end-use is handled as follows:

a) For the dhaba infrastructure portion, the bank plans to route payments directly to major contractors and equipment suppliers wherever feasible, based on approved estimates.

b) For the debt-consolidation component, Lokesh is required to provide account statements and settlement letters for each loan that is to be closed, within a defined timeline post-disbursement.

c) CAM(Credit Appraisal Memo) records that any fresh unsecured borrowing during the first three years of the LAP tenure must be pre-approved by the bank, failing which it may be treated as a breach of terms.

These measures ensure that the LAP genuinely improves the borrower's balance sheet rather than temporarily masking stress.

7.5 Collateral Risk

Even at the full ₹25 lakh, LTV remains around 55-56% on the ₹45 lakh valuation - well within internal policy. Yet, the property's semi-urban locality and 25 km distance from the branch could slow down realisation in an enforcement scenario under SARFAESI.

To mitigate this:

a) Very conservative valuation assumptions are adopted; forced-sale value is stress-tested internally.
b) The property is insured with bank clause, and all title documents and legal searches are checked meticulously.
c) The branch is instructed to periodically visit and record property condition as part of annual review.

7.6 Deviation Handling and Final Sanction Rationale

The sanctioning committee reviews the case with the following key points:

Strengths:

a) Long business vintage (10+ years) and stable cashflows.
b) Self-owned, litigation-free residential property with low LTV even at full requested amount.
c) Reasonable main applicant CIBIL of 730 and technical explanation for co-applicant's 626.

Concerns:

a) FOIR at ₹25 lakh well above normal and even above 65% deviation band based on current income.
b) KCC overdue and fully cash-based income.

After discussion, the committee concludes:

a) On a strict FOIR basis, eligibility would be limited to about ₹21-22 lakh.
b) However, post-renovation, dhaba seating is expected to increase materially, with potential for higher turnover, particularly on weekends and tourist seasons.
c) LTV remains very comfortable; property is in an improving locality; and formalising business turnover through banking channels will itself strengthen assessment over time.

Therefore, as a controlled exception, the bank sanctions the full ₹25 lakh LAP, but only with stringent conditions:

a) Clearance of ₹69,000 KCC overdue with documentary proof before disbursement.

b) Routing of at least 70% of dhaba receipts through the current account with Thar Gramin Bank, to be reviewed annually.

c) No new unsecured borrowings without prior written bank approval during the first three years.

d) Bank's right to call for partial prepayment if, during annual review, documented net income remains significantly below projections or FOIR exceeds a defined internal stress threshold.

The CAM(Credit Appraisal Memo) clearly records FOIR as the primary deviation, specifies approving authority, and states that this is a non-precedent, case-specific relaxation.

8. Outcome / Final Decision

The proposal is sanctioned for ₹25 lakh LAP with the above conditions. Disbursement is linked to KCC overdue clearance and, in stages, to infrastructure bills and debt-closure proofs. Over the next review cycle, Lokesh is expected to route higher volumes through the bank, enabling more data-driven assessment in future.

This case demonstrates that a credit officer must be able to separate what the numbers say, what policy allows, and where a justified, well-documented deviation can support business without compromising prudence.

9. Key Learnings for Credit Professionals

a) In cash-based SE-NP profiles, build income from ground realities (footfall, ticket size, days) and adopt conservative assumptions rather than relying on self-declared profits.

b) Treat FOIR as a hard risk metric: compute eligibility from income first, then compare with requested amount; deviations must be explicitly quantified and approved at the right level.

c) When ignoring obligations (short-tenor loans, KCCs) for FOIR, quote the exact policy clause and keep repayment track evidence on file to defend the decision later.

d) Investigate every bureau anomaly: obtain SOA, speak to lending branches, and distinguish between technical/reporting issues and genuine behavioural delinquencies.

e) Link sanction conditions to CIBIL and KCC issues - insist on full overdue clearance and documentary proof before disbursement to align with RBI's IRAC norms on overdues.

f) For LAP with mixed end-use, structure disbursement (direct vendor payments, proof-based debt closure) so that funds genuinely improve business capacity and borrower leverage.

g) Look beyond headline LTV - factor locality, distance from branch and legal enforceability when judging collateral strength and while setting monitoring frequency.

h) Write CAMs as self-contained narratives: any senior reading only your note should clearly understand business model, risk drivers, eligibility logic, deviations and sanction rationale without needing to refer back to PD notes or field worksheets.

•••

CASE STUDY 18

WHEN "FULLY SECURED" WAS AN ILLUSION: A TEXTILE WORKING CAPITAL FAILURE UNDER A WEAK DEED OF HYPOTHECATION

1. Introduction

In Indian banking, textile units are classic working capital customers, large inventories, extended receivable cycles, and heavy dependence on hypothecation of movable assets for securing cash credit limits. Generally, such facilities look "fully secured". In reality, the quality of the Deed of Hypothecation, its registration, and day-to-day monitoring can decide whether the bank finally recovers or ends up effectively unsecured.

This case study examines a mid-sized textile manufacturer financed primarily against hypothecated current assets and machinery. It traces how gaps in documentation, ROC/CERSAI filings, insurance, DP monitoring and condition enforcement slowly converted a seemingly well-secured exposure into a complex recovery case under SARFAESI.

2. Borrower / Business Background

Borrower: Navdurga Textiles Private Limited (NTPL).

Industry: Grey fabric weaving and processing.

Location: Rishivadi Industrial Cluster, Gujarat.

NTPL operates 120 power looms, a small processing unit (dyeing and finishing) and maintains substantial inventories of yarn, grey fabric, and finished fabric. The company sells to large garment exporters and domestic wholesalers on 60 - 90 days credit.

Turnover grew from ₹78 crore to ₹96 crore over three years, with moderate profitability but tight liquidity due to heavy stocking and elongated receivables in a competitive, price-sensitive market. The balance sheet reflected high current assets funded largely by bank borrowings and sundry creditors.

Promoters were first-generation entrepreneurs with strong technical knowledge but limited financial discipline. The company banked with Suraksha Bank Ltd. (SBL) as its sole banker for working capital for nearly eight years.

3. Type of Loan / Facility Details

SBL had sanctioned the following facilities to NTPL:

i) Cash Credit (Hypothecation of Stocks & Book Debts): ₹20 crore.

ii) Working Capital Term Loan (WCTL): ₹3 crore (to regularise overdue CC and creditors).

iii) Term Loan (Plant & Machinery): ₹4 crore (for new looms and processing machinery).

Primary Security:

i) Current Assets: Hypothecation of entire stocks of raw materials, WIP, finished goods, stores and spares, and book debts/receivables of NTPL, present and future.

ii) Movable Fixed Assets: Hypothecation of plant and machinery financed by the bank.

Collateral Security: Equitable mortgage of factory land and building owned by the promoter group company.

The security documents included a Master Facility Agreement, a Deed of Hypothecation for current assets and machinery, and a Mortgage Deed/ Memorandum of Entry for immovable property. The Deed of Hypothecation was executed on stamp paper at the then-prevailing rate in the state and contained a broad "all monies" clause covering present and future liabilities of NTPL to SBL.

4. Scenario & Developments

After a stable initial period, NTPL's business grew rapidly on the back of aggressive credit sales and bulk orders from a few large buyers. Based on rising turnover and projected orders, SBL enhanced the CC limit from ₹12 crore to ₹20 crore over four years and sanctioned the WCTL and machinery term loan during this period. The relationship was considered "strategic", and sanction time-lines were often compressed to meet borrower demands.

At the time of the first sanction, a Deed of Hypothecation was duly executed and registered with CERSAI and, being a company, the charge was filed with ROC within the prescribed timelines. However, during subsequent enhancements and the addition of WCTL, only a supplementary letter and revival of security documents were taken. No fresh or supplemental Deed of Hypothecation was executed clearly capturing the new limits, and the ROC/CERSAI records were not updated to reflect the enhanced exposure.

To manage rising raw material prices and discount-driven sales, NTPL started overstocking yarn and offering extended credit to a few large buyers. Stock statements showed high levels of inventory and receivables, and Drawing Power (DP) utilisation was consistently above 95%. On the surface, limits appeared "well backed" by current assets.

Over time, some stress signals emerged: increasing >120 day debtors, frequent requests for ad-hoc DP, cheques returned due to insufficient funds, and repeated delays in renewal data. On physical inspection, the branch occasionally found stock levels lower than reported but attributed it to "timing differences".

In the fifth year of the relationship, NTPL quietly availed additional working capital from a local NBFC, Shakumbhari Finlease Ltd., against hypothecation of certain machinery and stock. No formal NOC or second charge permission was obtained from SBL. Shakumbhari Finlease promptly registered its charge with CERSAI. SBL became aware of this only after stress turned acute.

A sudden fall in export orders, volatility in yarn prices and delayed collections from two major buyers caused severe cash flow problems. CC slipped into persistent irregularity, interest servicing became erratic, and statutory dues (especially GST and PF) started accumulating. Within six months, NTPL's account with SBL was classified as NPA.

5. Problem Statement

a) Was the Deed of Hypothecation and perfection of charge adequate to protect SBL's interest after multiple enhancements and additional facilities?

b) Did SBL's DP computation, stock-statement scrutiny and inspection practices truly reflect the quality and realisable value of the hypothecated current assets?

c) How serious was NTPL's violation of the negative lien and charge creation conditions in favour of Shakumbhari Finlease, and what should have been the appropriate response from SBL?

d) What risks arose from weak insurance controls, unpaid statutory dues and third-party (warehouse) interests over the same goods?

e) At NPA stage, how effectively could SBL enforce its floating charge that had crystallised into a fixed charge under SARFAESI, given competing claims and documentation gaps?

6. Detailed Analysis & Discussion

6.1 Adequacy of Deed of Hypothecation and Perfection of Charge

At the first sanction stage, SBL had done things correctly - a comprehensive Deed of Hypothecation was executed, adequately stamped, describing all present and future stocks, book debts and plant and machinery, with an "all monies" clause securing all current and future liabilities. The charge was registered with CERSAI and ROC within the statutory timelines, ensuring priority over subsequent creditors at that point.

The problem arose during later enhancements and the sanction of WCTL. Instead of executing a fresh or properly worded supplemental Deed of Hypothecation, the branch relied on a simple supplementary letter referring to the old deed, without clearly amending the secured amount and without updating ROC/CERSAI to reflect the higher exposure and additional facility. This created three risks:

i) In insolvency/liquidation, the liquidator or other creditors could argue that the registered charge amount did not fully cover the enhanced limits.

ii) The wording of the original deed, though broad, could be challenged for not specifically linking to the WCTL and fresh TL, especially if internal documentation also lacked clarity.

iii) The delay and omission in updating CERSAI provided room for subsequent lenders (like Shakumbhari Finlease) to establish and register their charges earlier in time for certain movable assets.

For the credit officer, the lesson was: execution of the Deed is not a one-time event; every material enhancement or structural change must be mapped into the security documentation and registrations, or the "secured" nature of exposure becomes vulnerable in court.

6.2 DP Computation, Stock Monitoring and Reality of Security

Throughout the relationship, stock statements submitted by NTPL showed apparently comfortable levels of inventory and receivables. DP calculations were done mechanically on the declared figures, with the standard margin applied.There was no rigorous comparison of:

- Monthly stock statements with audited/quarterly financials,
- Movement in key items (yarn, grey fabric, finished fabric) versus sales, or
- Age-wise debtor reports with actual realisation patterns.

During a late-stage stock audit ordered after the irregularities, several red flags surfaced like:

- A significant portion of debtors were actually over 180 days but were shown within 90 days.
- Obsolete and damaged fabric lying for more than a year was valued at full cost in stock statements.
- Substantial stock was lying in third-party godowns without clear documentation or tripartite control.

Effectively, while the bank had a legal hypothecation charge, the substance of security was weak - the realisable value of current assets was much lower than the DP against which funds were drawn. The Deed of Hypothecation(DoH) provided the legal backbone, but poor monitoring rendered the working capital exposure quasi-unsecured.

6.3 Breach of Negative Lien and Creation of Further Charge

The Deed of Hypothecation contained typical protective clauses prohibiting the borrower from creating further charge, lien or encumbrance over hypothecated assets without prior written consent of SBL, and requiring the borrower to keep assets free from adverse claims and encumbrances.

Despite this, NTPL availed finance from Shakumbhari Finlease, hypothecating portion of the same machinery and stock, and Shakumbhari promptly filed its charge with CERSAI. From a legal standpoint:

- NTPL clearly breached the negative lien/charge restriction clause in the DoH.
- SBL could have treated this as an event of default and recalled the facilities much earlier, preventing build-up of exposure and deterioration of assets.
- At enforcement, Shakumbhari Finlease argued that for specific machinery items and clearly tagged stock, its CERSAI registration was prior in time for those assets, leading to intense inter-creditor disputes.

The bank's laxity in tracking CERSAI registrations over its borrower and failure to react swiftly to this breach significantly weakened its practical control over security.

6.4 Insurance, Statutory Dues and Third-Party Interests

The DoH placed full responsibility on NTPL to insure hypothecated assets for adequate value, keep policies alive, and have the bank noted as sole loss payee. It also required timely payment of statutory dues and recognised that bank could not be responsible for third-party claims such as warehouse liens.

In practice:

a) Insurance policies were often renewed at lower values to save premium; in one year, finished goods were under-insured by almost 40%.

b) In the crucial year leading to default, there was a gap of nearly three weeks in policy renewal for stocks at a key hired godown.

c) GST and PF dues remained unpaid for several months, attracting potential "crown debt" and statutory priorities.

d) The main godown operator claimed unpaid storage charges for six months and asserted a lien over goods in his custody.

A minor fire incident occurred in the finishing section, damaging significant quantities of finished fabric. When the claim was lodged, the insurer raised issues on under-insurance and policy gaps, and delayed settlement. Ultimately, the claim amount was much lower than the actual loss. The reduced pay-out was applied partly to clear overdue premium and partly to SBL, leaving a substantial un-covered economic loss.

At the same time, during SARFAESI possession proceedings, the warehouse operator refused to release goods without payment of his dues, arguing a prior possessory lien. This further reduced the pool of readily realisable security for the bank.

6.5 Enforcement under SARFAESI and Crystallisation of Floating Charge

Upon NPA classification, SBL issued notice under Section 13(2) of the SARFAESI Act, 2002, calling upon NTPL to clear its dues. On non-compliance, SBL proceeded under Section 13(4) to take symbolic and then physical possession of the factory, plant and hypothecated movables.

Legally, as per the Deed of Hypothecation and Section 2(1)(n) of SARFAESI, the floating charge over stocks, receivables and machinery crystallised into a fixed charge on default - meaning NTPL no longer had the right to deal with those assets, and SBL could seize and sell them.

However, enforcement was complex:

a) Shakumbhari Finlease asserted its own hypothecation over specific machinery based on its charge documents and CERSAI registration, demanding a share in sale proceeds.

b) The warehouse operator sought settlement of his charges before releasing goods.

c) Two major buyers disputed quality and claimed set-off against receivables, reducing realisable book debts.

d) In ROC records, the registered charge amount in favour of SBL was lower than the then outstanding exposure, providing NTPL's counsel an argument (though weak) that part of the facility was not properly secured.

After protracted negotiations and multiple auctions, SBL could realise only about 45 - 50% of its total outstanding from sale of immovable and movable securities and partial insurance proceeds. The remaining exposure had to be partly recovered through a negotiated one-time settlement and partly written off.

7. Outcome / Final Decision

SBL's internal Credit Committee reviewed the entire case after partial recovery. The outcome and decisions were:

a) The account remained classified as NPA until closure under a negotiated settlement, with partial sacrifice approved at a higher committee level.

b) A portion of the outstanding was written off after adjusting all available securities, insurance claims and negotiated payments from the promoters.

c) Internal audit and vigilance departments highlighted serious lapses in security documentation updates, delayed ROC/CERSAI modifications, weak monitoring of borrower obligations and charge creation requirements (especially additional charge creation), and superficial scrutiny of stock statements.

d) The bank revised its internal credit policy to mandate fresh or supplemental Deed of Hypothecation and timely ROC/CERSAI updates for any material enhancement or new facility secured by the same assets.

e) Factory inspections were formalised with structured checklists, and periodic CERSAI searches were made compulsory at both sanction and annual review stages.

8. Key Lessons for Credit Professionals

a) **Treat the Deed of Hypothecation as a live risk document** - update it (and ROC/CERSAI) whenever limits are enhanced or new facilities are added, instead of relying on old wording and revival letters.

b) **Do not confuse legal hypothecation with real security** - validate stock statements, debtor ageing and DP through field inspections, stock audits and financial cross-checks, especially in inventory-heavy sectors like textiles.

c) **Monitor negative lien and additional charge aggressively** - periodic CERSAI searches and balance confirmation formats must capture whether the borrower has quietly created fresh charges elsewhere.

d) **Make insurance, statutory dues and third-party interests part of your core credit checklist** - under-insurance, unpaid GST/PF and warehouse liens can erode your practical priority over hypothecated assets.

e) **Understand and plan for crystallisation of floating charge** - once default signs appear, escalate early, tighten controls on stock movement, and be ready to quickly convert your floating charge into effective possession and sale under SARFAESI.

f) **Align sanction terms, DP policy and DoH wording** - ensure asset descriptions, margins and monitoring mechanisms all talk to each other, so that what looks "secured" on paper remains truly secured at enforcement stage.

Hypothecation Checklist – For Credit Managers

1. Always remember that hypothecation covers only movable property, existing and future, where possession stays with the borrower and only a charge is created in favour of the bank.
2. Ensure a properly stamped Deed of Hypothecation is executed whenever limits are sanctioned or enhanced against stocks, book debts or movable machinery, as per state stamp duty laws and bank policy.
3. Verify that the Deed of Hypothecation clearly identifies the lender, borrower/security provider, all sanctioned facilities and explicitly states the ranking of charge (first, pari passu, second, exclusive, etc.).
4. Check that the description of hypothecated assets covers all relevant present and future stocks, WIP, finished goods, consumables, spares and receivables, aligned with the business model and the base used for DP calculation.
5. Confirm that the Deed contains an all-monies clause so that the same security extends to all present and future liabilities of the borrower to the bank, not just a single limit.
6. For company borrowers, ensure ROC filing of the hypothecation charge is completed within the prescribed time after execution of the Deed and monitor any additional fees or compliances in case of delay.
7. Independently verify that the hypothecation charge has been correctly registered on CERSAI and that no prior or undisclosed charge exists on the same movable assets.
8. Ensure the borrower undertakes in the Deed not to create any further charge, lien, pledge or encumbrance on the hypothecated assets without the bank's prior written consent.
9. Scrutinise that the Deed places clear responsibility on the borrower to maintain the hypothecated goods in good, marketable and insurable condition and to bear all costs for their preservation, storage and protection.

10. Confirm that the insurance clause requires comprehensive cover on hypothecated assets with the bank noted as sole loss payee and empowers the bank to settle insurance claims directly with the insurer.
11. Check that the Deed obliges the borrower to maintain proper stock, debtor and invoice records, to allow inspection at any time, and to submit statements and information whenever demanded by the bank.
12. Ensure the Deed clearly allows the borrower to deal with hypothecated goods only in the ordinary course of business and requires routing of sale proceeds through the loan/CC account for proper churning and DP integrity.
13. Verify that the enforcement clause empowers the bank, on default, to enter premises, take possession, convert hypothecation into pledge, appoint a receiver, sell assets and appropriate proceeds towards all dues including costs.
14. Understand and confirm that the charge is drafted as a floating charge over present and future movables which crystallises into a fixed charge on occurrence of default or when the bank decides to enforce security.
15. In multiple banking or consortium cases, check that pari passu sharing, ranking of charge and lead bank documentation are properly reflected in the Deed and in CERSAI/ROC charge registrations.
16. Always cross-map key obligations in the Deed of Hypothecation, such as restriction on creation of additional charge, timely renewal of insurance, and accuracy of stock statements, into sanction conditions and internal rating triggers so that any breach automatically flags the account for prompt review and corrective action.
17. Document every stock inspection, factory visit and asset verification explicitly with reference to specific clauses of the Deed of Hypothecation so that, at the time of SARFAESI or wilful default proceedings, the bank can demonstrate clear contractual breaches supported by contemporaneous evidence.

•••

CASE STUDY 19

WHEN DSCR LIES: UNMASKING INFLATED CASH ACCRUALS, PERSONAL OBLIGATIONS AND RECEIVABLE STRESS IN A SERVICE-SECTOR LAP

1. Introduction

This case study explores how a strong service-sector borrower, backed by a good credit bureau score and a high-value commercial property, ended up struggling to service a Loan Against Property (LAP) within eighteen months of sanction.

The case focuses on how improper computation of Debt Service Coverage Ratio (DSCR), ignorance of non-operating and non-cash items, and inadequate assessment of personal obligations can seriously distort a lender's perception of repayment capacity. It also focuses on the importance of analysing cash flows and debtor days even in service businesses, not just manufacturing or trading.

2. Borrower / Business Background

The borrower is Midas Advisory Services, a partnership firm based in the city of Jamnagar. The firm provides corporate consulting and technology implementation support to mid-sized manufacturing and trading entities.

Key features of the business:

a) **Partners:** Two professionals, both qualified MBAs with prior corporate experience.

b) **Business model:** Project-based consulting assignments with phased billing and milestone-based payments, along with a small annuity-style retainer base.

c) **Revenue pattern:** Lumpy cash flows with high concentration in top five clients.

d) **Historical performance:**

  - Turnover grew from ₹4.20 crore to ₹7.80 crore over three years.
  - Profit Before Tax (PBT) reported in the latest audited year: ₹82 lakh.
  - Net Profit After Tax (PAT): ₹60 lakh.
  - Balance sheet showed low fixed assets and relatively high trade receivables.

e) **Personal profile:** Both partners also have personal home loans and vehicle loans. Some EMIs are paid from the firm's bank account under the umbrella of "partners' drawings".

At first glance, the business appears profitable, professionally run, and housed in a self-owned commercial property in a prime commercial complex.

3. Type of Loan / Facility Details

Midas Advisory Services approached Suryodaya Bank Ltd. (a fictional bank) for a Loan Against Property (Business Purpose).

Key terms of the LAP:

i) **Facility:** Term Loan against equitable mortgage of self-owned commercial office premises.

ii) **Purpose:**
  - Takeover of an existing high-cost LAP from another NBFC.
  - Additional top-up for business expansion (hiring more consultants, upgrading IT infrastructure, and providing additional working capital buffer).

iii) **Property:** Commercial office space of 3,000 sq. ft. in "Prime Plaza", Jamnagar.
  - Market valuation by bank's empanelled valuer: ₹3.60 crore.
  - Approved LTV: 60%.

iv) **Sanctioned Term Loan:** ₹2.10 crore.

v) **Tenor:** 10 years.

vi) **Interest rate:** Floating, linked to internal MCLR + spread.

vii) **Repayment:** Equated Monthly Instalments (EMIs).

At appraisal stage, the credit team relied heavily on DSCR and net profit figures to justify the sanction, considering LAP as a relatively "safer" product due to collateral comfort.

4. Scenario / Developments

For the first six months, the account appeared satisfactory. EMIs were paid on time, and the current account showed healthy turnover.

However, after about nine months, the following developments emerged:

a) EMIs started getting delayed by 10–15 days and occasionally bounced once before being cleared.

b) The current account reflected decreasing average monthly credits, with long periods of low balance.

c) Trade receivables increased sharply, both in absolute amount and in debtor days.

d) Partners began requesting ad hoc overdraft facilities and temporary deferment of EMIs, citing "delayed client payments" and "slowdown in the consulting market".

A detailed review was initiated at the Regional Office, where the credit officer re-examined the original appraisal, cash flows, and DSCR computation.

5. Problem Statement

On deeper analysis, four core issues emerged:

a) **Inflated DSCR at Sanction Stage:** The original DSCR had been calculated using Net Profit plus depreciation and non-operating income, without eliminating exceptional items or recognising that some components were one-time gains. This resulted in an artificially high DSCR which overstated the true debt-servicing capacity of the firm.

b) **Hidden Personal Obligations and Excessive Drawings:** The firm's bank statements revealed that EMIs of the partners' personal home loan and car loans were regularly debited from the firm's account and recorded as "drawings". While these did not appear as business finance cost, they significantly reduced the cash actually available to service the LAP EMI.

c) **Deterioration in Debtor Days and Operating Cycle:** Although the borrower operated in the service sector, trade receivables were high and rising. Debtor days had increased from around 75 days to nearly 140 days, indicating slower collections, client concentration risk, and cash flow stress. This change had not been adequately factored into the projections at the time of sanction.

d) **LAP Used as Quasi–Working Capital & Debt Consolidation Tool:** A significant portion of the top-up component of the LAP was effectively being used to plug working capital gaps and refinance personal obligations. The structure had, therefore, combined business funding, personal refinancing, and takeover of earlier high-cost debt into a single term loan, increasing long-term leverage without a commensurate and sustainable improvement in earnings.

6. Detailed Analysis & Discussion

6.1 How DSCR Was Originally Computed

At sanction stage, the credit note showed an average projected DSCR of 1.75, which was considered comfortable as per the bank's internal norms (minimum 1.50).

The computation was broadly as follows for the most recent year:

Reported PAT: ₹60 lakh

Add: Depreciation: ₹10 lakh

Add: Interest on existing LAP and small vehicle loan: ₹18 lakh

Add: One-time profit on sale of old furniture and equipment: ₹12 lakh

Cash Accruals = ₹60 lakh + ₹10 lakh + ₹18 lakh + ₹12 lakh = ₹1.00 crore

DSCR = Cash Accruals / Total Annual Debt Obligation

Total annual debt obligation (interest + instalment) for the proposed LAP was around ₹57 lakh, giving a DSCR of about 1.75.

However, this calculation had multiple weaknesses:

a) Non-operating and one-time income (profit on sale of assets) was treated as if it were regular income.

b) Depreciation was correctly added back, but there was no adjustment for exceptional or non-recurring expenses.

c) Most importantly, the appraisal failed to recognise that family drawings and personal EMIs, paid from the same bank account, would reduce the actual surplus available for servicing the LAP.

From a conceptual standpoint, "profit available for lenders" should be calculated by focusing on sustainable operating profit, adding back non-cash expenses like depreciation, and eliminating non-operating and exceptional items.

6.2 Reassessment of Profit from Normal Business Operations

During the review, the credit officer reworked the numbers using the audited P&L and bank statements.

Key adjustments included:

a) Profit on sale of fixed assets (₹12 lakh) was treated as non-operating and removed from the numerator for DSCR; it was recognised as a one-time gain.

b) Certain exceptional consulting income booked under a special "advisory success fee" for a single large client, which was unlikely to recur, was moderated in forward projections.

d) Depreciation (₹10 lakh) was added back as a non-cash expense, which was appropriate, but the officer also identified that substantial "provisions" were largely prudential and did not involve immediate cash outflow. After applying conservative judgment, only a portion was added back.

e) Average annual partners' drawings, including EMIs routed through the firm's account, were estimated at about ₹30 lakh per annum and treated as outflows that reduce the surplus available for loan servicing.

Once these adjustments were made, the effective cash surplus from the core business available for servicing the LAP and other term obligations was closer to ₹70 - ₹72 lakh rather than the ₹1.00 crore originally assumed.

With total annual debt obligation (existing and proposed) of about ₹57 lakh, the revised DSCR was only around 1.25 - 1.30, and that too based on a year which had unusually strong performance. Projected DSCR for subsequent years, factoring in rising receivable days and modest growth, fell even further.

6.3 Deterioration in Debtor Days and Cash Flow Impact

While LAP is a term loan against property, its repayment still ultimately depends on business cash flows in this case, because the property is a productive business asset and promoters are not in a position to infuse large external funds.

The officer analysed receivables trend over three years:

Year 1: Debtor days - 80

Year 2: Debtor days - 95

Year 3 (latest): Debtor days around 135–140

For a consulting firm that claims 60 - 75 days credit terms, this trend was alarming. It indicated that:

a) Clients were taking longer to pay, possibly bargaining harder or delaying due to their own stress.
b) The firm was increasingly relying on extended credit and "faith-based" client relationships rather than strict commercial discipline.
c) Cash remained locked in receivables, forcing the promoter to use the LAP top-up portion and available cash to bridge working capital gaps instead of creating real growth.

The rising operating cycle effectively converted what should have been a relatively comfortable DSCR into a fragile one, highly sensitive to any delay in a few large invoices.

6.4 LAP as a Quasi–Working Capital and Debt Consolidation Tool

Though the stated purpose of LAP was "business expansion and takeover of existing loan", the actual utilisation pattern revealed that:

- About half of the top-up amount was used to clear informal high-cost borrowings and credit card dues of the partners.
- A portion went into funding receivables (pending client payments) and clearing overdue obligations to vendors and consultants.
- Only a limited amount was invested in genuine growth initiatives such as technology upgrade or hiring.

This is a common phenomenon: LAP is often treated as a multi-purpose consolidation tool because the EMI per lakh looks lower and tenor is longer. From a prudential point of view, however, this raises serious concerns:

- Long-term collateral-backed debt is being used to fund short-term working capital needs.
- Personal and business obligations get mixed, making it hard to correctly assess DSCR and cash flow sufficiency.
- Any adverse business cycle movement immediately affects LAP servicing, despite apparently "strong" collateral.

While RBI's general guidance emphasises that cash flow, not collateral, should be the primary basis for credit decisions, in this case the appraisal had leaned heavily on property value and bureau scores instead of cash flow robustness.

6.5 Risk, Regulatory Angle and Possible Corrective Measures

From a regulatory standpoint, the account had not yet turned NPA under IRAC norms, but warning signals were clearly visible:

- EMI bouncing and overdues.
- Increasing receivables and elongating operating cycle.
- Declining net surplus after partners' drawings.
- Overdependence on a few large clients.

The Regional Office considered the following options:

i) Tight monitoring and partial restructuring

- Restructure was not immediately invoked, as that would attract regulatory implications and downgrades.
- Instead, the bank explored reducing the EMI by marginally extending the loan tenor (within policy limits), along with imposing a clear condition prohibiting any further drawdowns and informal borrowing.

ii) Business discipline and borrower obligations

- The borrower was advised to implement stricter credit control, including clear credit periods and follow-up systems to reduce debtor days.
- The bank stipulated that the borrower must periodically submit age-wise debtor statements and provide quarterly CA-certified DSCR

calculations, ensuring that the ratio remains above the prescribed minimum threshold.

iii) Segregation of personal and business obligations

- Partners were formally advised to route personal EMIs through their individual savings accounts instead of the firm's current account.
- Future assessment was anchored around business cash flows after reasonable drawings but before debt servicing, to align with the true spirit of DSCR and FOIR concepts.

7. Outcome / Final Decision

After detailed discussion with the borrower, the bank opted for a measured corrective approach rather than immediate hard action:

i) Tenor was marginally extended within board-approved norms, reducing the EMI to a level more consistent with realistic DSCR. No formal restructuring classification was triggered, but the account was tagged for "early warning" monitoring.

ii) The bank documented clear action points for the borrower, including targeted reduction in debtor days from 140 to below 100 over the next twelve months, and diversification of client base to reduce dependence on top three clients.

iii) A quarterly review mechanism was introduced, covering:

- Updated financials and provisional P&L
- Age-wise receivable analysis
- Revised DSCR calculations, stripping out non-operating and exceptional items
- Verification that partners' personal EMIs are no longer routed from the firm's account

Over the next year, the account stabilised but did not become as strong as originally projected. While EMIs were serviced more regularly, it became clear that the case would have been structured and priced differently had the initial DSCR and cash flow analysis been done prudently.

8. Key Lessons for Credit Professionals

a) Always compute DSCR based on sustainable operating profit, adding back only genuine non-cash expenses and eliminating non-operating, exceptional and one-time items from the numerator.

b) Treat partners' drawings, personal EMIs, and family lifestyle expenses as real cash outflows that reduce the surplus available for debt servicing, especially in proprietorships and partnership firms.

c) In service-sector LAPs, rigorously track debtor days and client concentration; elongating receivable cycles and dependence on a few large clients are early warning signals that can rapidly erode DSCR.

d) Do not allow LAP to become a catch - all refinancing tool for working capital gaps and personal debt consolidation without explicitly modelling the impact on long-term cash flows and leverage.

e) Anchor credit decisions on cash flow viability - not on collateral value alone and institutionalise periodic post-sanction reviews of DSCR, operating cycle, and utilisation patterns to detect stress well before an account turns NPA.

•••

CASE STUDY 20

FROM PROMOTER DEATH TO PROMOTER INTENT, READING THE CREDIT SIGNALS RIGHT

A ₹6.5 Crore Working Capital Decision under High Inventory, Sticky Debtors and Succession Risk

1. Introduction

A mid-sized engineering unit, Aarya Mobility Components Pvt Ltd (AMCPL), approaches Pragati Bank Ltd for a takeover and enhancement of working capital facilities. On paper, the account reflects stressed repayment history, high stock days, sticky debtors, near-full limit utilisation and a recent turnover dip.

However, a deeper appraisal, including unit visit, reference checks and conservative adjustments forces the credit officer to decide whether this is a case of genuine temporary stress with strong promoter intent, or a structurally weak, over-leveraged account that should be avoided.

2. Borrower / Business Background

Aarya Mobility Components Pvt Ltd (AMCPL) is a closely held private limited company based in Muzzafarnagar Industrial Estate, a Tier-2 city in North India.

Business activity: Manufacturing of precision fasteners, brackets and structural components used in two-wheelers and light commercial vehicles.

Customers: i) Tier-1 vendors supplying to leading OEMs in India. ii) Direct export to aftermarket distributors in Europe and the Middle East.

Suppliers: Large domestic steel manufacturers and importers of alloy steel.

The business was started in 2012 by Mr. Rajiv Bhaskar, a first-generation entrepreneur.

In February 2021, Rajiv died suddenly due to a cardiac arrest. His daughter, Ms. Kavya Bhaskar, then a 21-year-old engineering student, stepped in as

Managing Director, supported by her mother (a homemaker and non-executive director) and a professional CFO.

The family owns an industrial land and building (factory) in the company's name. The property is already mortgaged to Pragati Bank's Retail Asset Centre for a Loan Against Property (LAP) availed by the company prior to Rajiv's demise.

3. Type of Loan / Facility Details

AMCPL currently enjoys the following facilities with Suryodaya Bank Ltd (existing banker):

a) Cash Credit (Hypothecation of stock & receivables) - ₹3.50 crore

b) Letter of Credit (LC) for raw material imports - ₹1.00 crore

In addition, the company has:

a) LAP from Pragati Bank (Retail Asset Centre) - Outstanding ₹1.80 crore, secured by first charge on factory land and building (valuation: ₹6.00 crore).

b) Small channel finance / vendor bill discounting limits of about ₹0.70 crore with an NBFC.

AMCPL has now approached Pragati Bank - SME Division with the following request:

1) Takeover of Cash Credit of ₹3.50 crore from Suryodaya Bank, and

2) Enhancement of total working capital limits to ₹6.50 crore, structured as:

Cash Credit (Stock + Debtors): ₹5.00 crore

LC (Import / Purchase of steel): ₹1.50 crore

Security structure proposed:

Primary: Hypothecation of stocks and book debts.

Collateral: Extension of equitable mortgage over existing factory land & building (already mortgaged to Pragati Bank for LAP), with pari-passu charge between LAP and WC, ensuring overall LTV within internal policy norms.

4. Scenario and Recent Developments

Financial Performance (₹ crore)

Particulars	FY23	FY24	FY25	FY26 (Proj)
Turnover	34	42	39	44
EBITDA Margin	6.5%	7.8%	8.5%	8.5%
PAT Margin	1.2%	1.5%	1.3%	1.4%
Net Worth (Adj)*	11.0	12.5	12.0	11.8
Total Funded Debt	6.5	8.7	9.5	9.8

*Adjusted for related-party deposits; further conservative adjustments discussed later.

Working Capital Position - FY25

Stock: ₹12.0 crore → approx. 270 days holding (on ₹39 crore turnover).

Debtors: ₹5.8 crore → 55–60 days (excluding certain sticky receivables).

Creditors: ₹4.0 crore → 90–95 days.

Channel finance utilisation: 70 - 80%.

CC utilisation: Averaging 92 - 95% throughout the year.

Stress Points Visible on File

a) LAP EMI Bounces / CIBIL DPD

- From April 2022 to December 2023, most LAP EMIs bounced at least once before being cleared.
- CIBIL reflects multiple DPD buckets (30 - 60 days) during this period.

b) Old Business Loan Closure

- The company had an unsecured business loan from an NBFC (₹0.75 crore) which also reflected frequent EMI bounces.
- This was closed in mid-2024 from a life insurance claim received after Rajiv's demise.

c) Turnover Dip & H1(First half) Performance

- Turnover dropped from ₹42 crore (FY24) to ₹39 crore (FY25).
- For H1 FY26, turnover is ₹16 crore vs ₹20 crore in H1 FY23 - a ~20% dip, largely from export side due to soft demand in Europe.

d) **Sticky Debtors**

- Around ₹1.2 crore of receivables are over 12 months old, partly under dispute for quality claims and pricing differences.

e) **LC Devolvement & Cheque Returns**

- Suryodaya Bank's statement shows two instances of LC devolvement during FY25, each regularised within 7 - 10 days.
- Around 18 inward cheque returns >₹1 lakh are observed during the year, mainly in a smaller current account of the company.

f) **Very High Stock Days**

- Stock holding of 270 days seems abnormally high for an auto-component business, raising suspicion about stock inflation or slow-moving inventory.

Given these red flags, the appraisal team at Pragati Bank SME Division flags the case for a detailed credit assessment and unit visit before taking a call on the takeover and enhancement.

5. Problem Statement

a) How should the bank interpret the stressed LAP and NBFC EMI track, especially given the promoter transition after Rajiv's death?

b) Is the requested ₹6.5 crore working capital exposure justified in light of the recent turnover dip, high overall leverage and near-full utilisation of limits?

c) Are the extremely high stock days (270) a symptom of a flawed business model / stock inflation, or a legitimate requirement of the company's operating model?

d) How should the bank treat the sticky debtors of ₹1.2 crore (>12 months) from a risk and monitoring perspective?

e) Do the LC devolvements and cheque bounces indicate structural cashflow weakness, or are they isolated operational issues that can be mitigated?

e) Is the proposed security structure with factory property already mortgaged for LAP – legally and prudentially adequate for the enhanced working capital facilities?

6. Detailed Analysis

6.1 Promoter Quality, Succession and EMI Track

The EMI bounces on LAP and NBFC loans create a negative first impression. Under RBI's IRAC norms, any EMI overdue >30 days would move into SMA-1 category; persistent stress would typically trigger early warning signals.

However, the timeline of events is crucial:

- Rajiv's sudden death in Feb 2021 coincided with Covid lockdowns, severe demand disruption and operational dislocation.
- For nearly 18 months, the family struggled with both personal and business shocks, while Kavya was still completing her degree and had not fully entered operations.
- During this time, EMIs were often paid manually after bouncing, reflecting cashflow strain and weak financial discipline, but not complete delinquency.

The situation materially changed in mid-2024:

- The life insurance claim of nearly ₹1.0 crore was received.
- The family used this to fully close the NBFC business loan and clear all overdues and penalties, rather than seeking waivers.
- LAP EMIs have been regular since April 2024, with the mandate shifted from Rajiv's old account to AMCPL's main current account and Kavya's personal account as backup.

This behaviour displays positive intent: when liquidity became available, they chose to regularise and deleverage, not to walk away. For an experienced credit officer, this is a strong indicator that past stress was event-driven, not structurally fraudulent or malafide.

6.2 Business Model, Turnover Trend and Leverage

AMCPL operates as a high-variety, medium-volume component manufacturer. Each customer has custom made specifications and expects short lead times.

Turnover pattern:

- Post-Covid, the company recovered from ₹34 crore (FY23) to ₹42 crore (FY24), then slipped to ₹39 crore (FY25).

- Break-up shows that domestic OEM-linked sales have been stable, while export aftermarket sales fell sharply in H2 FY25 due to soft demand and inventory correction in Europe.
- H1 FY26 at ₹16 crore seems weak vs ₹20 crore in H1 FY25, but order book and confirmed schedules from OEMs and export clients suggest better H2 FY26 visibility.

Debt profile:

- Total funded debt FY25: ₹9.5 crore (LAP + WC + NBFC channel finance).
- Debt / Cash Accrual ≈ 9x (cash accrual ~₹1.05 crore).
- DSCR on term obligations remains around 1.35x - 1.40x.
- Current ratio (including stock at book) ~1.45:1, above traditional MPBF benchmark of 1.33:1.

While leverage is on the higher side for this size of company, it is not yet in the unsustainable zone, especially given:

- Reasonable DSCR,
- Tangible net worth >₹12 crore, and
- Presence of hard collateral.

However, the combination of high debt + high inventory + sticky debtors mandates a conservative stance and tight post-sanction monitoring.

6.3 High Stock Days - Red Flag or Business Model?

The most alarming number is inventory of 270 days. For many industries, RBI's broad working capital guidelines and internal bank policies consider 90–180 days a normal range.

During the unit visit, the credit team observed:

a) A fully integrated plant: wire drawing, forging, machining, heat treatment and surface finishing under one roof.

b) Stock largely comprised semi-finished and finished components for long-standing customers, backed by historical off-take patterns and annual schedules.

c) Steel sections and rods stacked in clearly demarcated zones; limited visible scrap or rusted/non-moving material.

d) Around 200–225 workers on the shop floor and multiple CNC/forging lines running in two shifts.

Kavya explained that AMCPL's competitive advantage lies in short turnaround time (TAT):

a) OEMs and overseas buyers place call-off orders with tight delivery timelines.
b) AMCPL pre-produces standard variants for key customers, using historical consumption data, so that orders can be executed in 4 - 6 weeks, whereas competitors take 3–4 months.
c) The steel used is re-usable and re-meltable, so risk of absolute obsolescence is contained.

Given this evidence, the 270 days stock appears model-driven, not fabricated. Nevertheless, from a prudential standpoint:

- The bank decides to cap drawing power eligibility at 240 days of raw + WIP + finished goods for DP calculations, to add a buffer against potential overstatement.
- The balance 30 days effectively becomes promoter-funded margin, strengthening overall risk comfort.

This balances business reality with risk control.

6.4 Sticky Debtors - Conservative Adjustments

The ₹1.2 crore debtors outstanding for more than 12 months are a clear warning signal. Some balances are in dispute over alleged quality issues; others reflect small overseas customers facing liquidity problems.

The credit officer adopts a conservative approach:

- Treats ₹1.0 crore out of ₹1.2 crore as fully irrecoverable for appraisal purposes.
- Reduces adjusted net worth from ₹12.0 crore to ₹11.0 crore.
- Reclassifies this amount as non-current / doubtful in internal ratio calculations, removing it from DP-eligible book debts.

Even after this haircut:

- Net worth remains >₹11 crore.
- Current ratio (on adjusted figures) remains >1.33:1.

Sanction conditions include:

- Time-bound recovery / write-off plan for the sticky receivables.
- No further credit allowed to customers who form part of this sticky bucket.

This approach aligns with RBI's emphasis on prudence, transparency and conservative provisioning, even in pre-NPA stages.

6.5 LC Devolvement and Cheque Returns - Context Matters

Two LC devolvements during FY25 and 18 cheque returns initially suggest liquidity stress. However, deeper analysis reveals:

a) Both devolved LCs were cleared within 7 - 10 days, funded by receivables; there was no roll-over or conversion into funded interest term loans.

b) Written confirmation from Suryodaya Bank asserts that there is no instance of LC remaining overdue beyond 30 days, hence no NPA-triggering devolvement.

c) Cheque returns are concentrated in a smaller current account used for secondary collections and incidental payments; the main CC account shows far fewer returns and generally adequate balance.

Thus, while these are undoubtedly EWS (Early Warning Signals), they are not of a magnitude that would justify outright rejection. Instead, they justify:

a) A condition of minimum average quarterly balance in the CC account.

b) Routing of at least 80–85% of sales through Pragati Bank post-takeover.

c) Quarterly review of cheque return trends as part of monitoring.

6.6 Security Structure, Legal Comfort and Regulatory Perspective

The factory land and building valued at ₹6.0 crore are already mortgaged to Pragati Bank's Retail Asset Centre for LAP. Post-sanction, the bank proposes:

a) Pari-passu mortgage between LAP and WC facilities.

b) Overall exposure of the bank (LAP + WC) at about ₹8.3 crore against property value of ₹6.0 crore plus current assets under hypothecation.

From a security and legal standpoint:

a) A common mortgage deed / amended memorandum of entry will clearly record pari-passu charge, ensuring enforceability under SARFAESI Act, 2002 for both LAP and WC in case of default.

b) ROC charge modification will reflect the enhanced and shared charge in favour of Pragati Bank.

While LTV on collateral alone is slightly high, the bank's overall comfort is derived from:

a) Combined value of property + current assets,

b) Verified business operations and franchise strength, and

c) Conservative haircuts applied on debtors and stock in internal assessment.

The proposal, therefore, meets internal credit policy and general RBI prudential expectations on secured MSME lending, subject to strong ongoing monitoring.

7. Outcome / Final Credit Decision

After combining financial analysis, promoter assessment, business model evaluation, security comfort and regulatory considerations, the sanctioning authority at Pragati Bank takes a measured positive call:

Sanction approved for:

Cash Credit (Hypothecation) - ₹5.00 crore

LC Limit - ₹1.50 crore

Takeover of Suryodaya Bank's CC is to be executed only after:

a) Confirmation of account being Standard,

b) No devolved LC or overdue interest as on takeover date, and

c) No pending SMA classification at the existing bank.

Key sanction conditions include:

a) Mandatory routing of at least 85% of total sales through Pragati Bank accounts.

b) Stock and book debt statements monthly; DP to be calculated with:
   - Stock capped at 240 days,
   - Exclusion of sticky debtors >180 days.

c) No further unsecured borrowing or NBFC limits without prior written approval.

d) Capital expenditure beyond ₹50 lakh to be undertaken only from internal accruals or specifically approved term loans.

e) Quarterly review of turnover, inventory days, debtor ageing and cheque return position; breach of agreed thresholds to trigger risk rating downgrade / corrective action.

f) Maintenance of minimum DSCR of 1.30x on overall term obligations.

8. Key Lessons for Credit Professionals

a) **Always align numbers with narrative and timeline** - EMI bounces and DPD must be read along with life events (death of promoter, Covid, etc.) and subsequent corrective actions to separate temporary shock from chronic weakness.

b) **Promoter intent is revealed by how they use liquidity** - voluntarily closing high-cost or stressed loans and regularising dues (even with full penal charges) is a strong indicator of ethical repayment culture.

c) **High inventory is not automatically bad** - for certain models (pre-production for key customers, export-led manufacturing), high stock days may be a strategic moat, provided it is verified through unit visits, process understanding and physical inspection.

d) **Treat sticky receivables with ruthless conservatism** - apply haircuts, remove them from DP, adjust net worth and build structured recovery conditions into the sanction; this protects the bank while still allowing viable borrowers to grow.

e) **Interpret LC devolvements and cheque returns in context** - Assess the frequency, regularisation period, and concentration; isolated or low-materiality instances can be addressed through structured monitoring conditions and corrective undertakings rather than outright rejection.

f) **Security comfort must be holistic, not just LTV-driven** - combine collateral value, quality and control over current assets, plus structural and legal enforceability under SARFAESI, to arrive at genuine risk comfort.

g) **Risk-based structuring and monitoring are as important as sanctioning** - limits, sub-limits, DP caps, routing conditions and periodic reviews should be designed to actively contain and track risk, not merely satisfy documentation requirements.

h) **A good credit decision is defendable, not perfect** - the objective is not to eliminate all risk, but to take well-understood, well-priced and well-documented risk, backed by realistic assumptions and clear articulation of both vulnerabilities and mitigants.

•••

CASE STUDY 21

KASAVU ILLUSIONS IN ERNAKULAM: HOW A 'PERFECT' SAREE BUSINESS EXPOSED DEEP WORKING CAPITAL, GST AND INTEGRITY RISKS AT KERALA DEVELOPMENT BANK

1. Introduction

Kerala Development Bank (KDB) received an attractive proposal from a well-known Ernakulam-based Kasavu saree business, "Malabar Kasavu Creations" (MKC).

The case came through the bank's SME & Wealth vertical, which positioned it as a "high-potential ethnic wear brand" with strong collateral, good CIBIL scores, and robust festival-driven sales. The branch, impressed by the unit's showroom and the promoter's local reputation, was keen to onboard the relationship quickly.

However, when the Credit Team at the Zonal Office began a detailed appraisal, a very different story started emerging. What initially looked like a high-quality ₹6 crore relationship for KDB slowly unfolded as a classic example of engineered turnover, working capital over-funding, diversion of funds, dual banking, and serious integrity concerns.

2. Borrower & Business Background

Malabar Kasavu Creations (MKC) is a private limited company based in Ernakulam, Kerala. The company is engaged in:

a) Manufacturing, finishing and trading of traditional Kasavu sarees and mundus

b) Supplying to wholesale traders in Thrissur, Kochi and Gulf-export houses

c) Running a small retail showroom near Ernakulam South

Promoter profile

Mr. Vishnu Nair (38) - Commerce graduate, front-facing promoter and managing director.

Mrs. Devika Nair (35) - Non-executive director, involved in design and social media branding.

A network of "job-work" weavers and small powerloom units in and around Aluva and Chalakkudy.

The promoter family has been in textiles for years. However, ROC search shows that Vishnu's father, Mr. Narayanan Nair, was earlier a director in a company called Kerala Heritage Silks Pvt. Ltd., which has large unpaid dues with multiple banks and is reflected in MSME default records.

MKC itself is only in its second full financial year of operations, but the promoters claim to have "decades of experience" via their erstwhile proprietary concerns.

3. Type of Loan / Facility Details

MKC approached Kerala Development Bank - Ernakulam SME Branch with the following requirements:

a) Working Capital (Cash Credit):

- Takeover of existing CC of ₹4.00 crore from a PSU bank (Coastal State Bank), and
- Enhancement to ₹4.50 crore (stock + book-debt based DP).

b) Term Loan (Machinery & Renovation):

- Fresh ₹1.50 crore to upgrade looms, dyeing unit and showroom interiors.

Total proposed exposure: ₹6.00 crore

Primary Security proposed

- Hypothecation of stock and book-debts.
- First charge on plant & machinery.

Collateral offered

- Commercial building (factory + showroom) near Aluva - stated value ₹7 - 8 crore.
- Additionally, promoter later "offered" a newly constructed luxury villa near Fort Kochi to strengthen comfort (title in personal name).

Existing limits at Coastal State Bank: CC ₹4.00 crore & Machinery TL ₹1.20 crore (outstanding ₹1.05 crore). No CGTMSE was applicable on MKC itself due to exposure size, but Vishnu also had smaller CGTMSE-backed business loans in his proprietary trading concern.

4. Scenario & Developments

On the surface, the case looked excellent:

a) CIBIL scores of both Vishnu and Devika above 760.

b) No reported overdues or write-offs.

c) GST returns showing FY 2024-25 turnover of ₹17.80 crore, FY 2025-26 (provisional) at ₹18.50 crore.

d) Existing CC conduct, as per CA's summary, "satisfactory".

e) Attractive factory premises, modern looms, and a tastefully done retail showroom.

f) Promoter maintaining a decent mutual fund and NRE deposit portfolio with KDB's Wealth division.

The branch saw it as: Full collateral cover + strong ethnic brand + high turnover + cross-sell potential = ideal SME case.

But the Credit Team insisted on:

a) Full 12-month bank statements from Coastal State Bank

b) One-year current account statements from other banks

c) GST returns with HSN-wise sales

d) ROC search, MCA/ProB checks on group entities/relatives

e) Unit visit before in-principle clearance

The deeper they went, the more the comfort eroded.

5. Problem Statement

After preliminary analysis, the Credit Team crystallised following key problem areas that needed to be addressed before any sanction could be considered:

a) Suspicion of engineered turnover and round-tripping through closely related parties.

b) Mismatch between claimed Kasavu saree manufacturing model and actual GST/HSN patterns, along with abnormal seasonality.

c) Over-funding risk when true working capital requirement was recalculated on realistic turnover and cycle assumptions.

d) Inflated stock and understatement of creditors in DP statements, along with ineligible group debtors being taken for drawing power.

e) Diversion of working capital funds towards a personal luxury villa, followed by an attempt to use the same property as collateral.

f) Integrity and transparency concerns: family default history, refusal to share full group financials/give corporate guarantee, and multiple high-cost business loans.

g) Dual banking and routing behaviour, plus a worrying gap between on-paper operations and ground reality observed during the unit visit.

6. Detailed Analysis & Discussion

6.1 Business Model vs Seasonality vs Actual Data

Kasavu sarees are inherently seasonal:

- Production & procurement: usually from January to July
- Peak billing & dispatch: July-September (Onam & wedding season)
- Collections: typically September-December, sometimes into January

If MKC is genuinely doing around ₹18 crore annual sales primarily in Kasavu sarees, the banking pattern should show fairly smooth churning from March to October, with some tapering post-season.

However, when the 12-month bank statement of Coastal State Bank was analysed, the pattern was quite different:

a) Around 80-85% of total annual credits were concentrated in three short bursts :
   - Mid-April to early May.
   - Late August to mid-September.
   - A brief window in December.

b) On several days, there were large round-figure credits and almost matching debits on the same day

c) Outside these bursts, the account remained relatively quiet, with small payments and housekeeping entries

On GST analysis, it was further observed that:

A disproportionate percentage of billed turnover in those bursts was towards two entities:

- Nair Ethnic Exports LLP.
- Nair Textiles Traders.

Both had common family surnames and appeared to be group/related concerns. Purchases too showed a mirror pattern with these entities or their connected parties.

For a genuine Kasavu manufacturer, one expects a wider base of retailers/ wholesalers, not such heavy concentration with two related parties. This pattern strongly suggested that a significant portion of billed turnover was engineered, not real third-party business.

6.2 GST & HSN Mismatch with Claimed Activity

From the unit visit and promoter interaction, the declared narrative was:

"We are primarily a Kasavu saree and mundu manufacturer, with some fabric trading only as a side activity."

But the HSN-wise GST report revealed that:

a) A substantial portion of outward supplies (by value) was under generic cotton fabric / grey cloth HSNs,

b) While supplies under finished saree/garment HSN codes were significantly lower than expected for a "pure saree manufacturer."

This indicated that MKC was likely doing more fabric rotation and trading than actual value-added Kasavu manufacturing. The retail branding was more of a façade.

When the team probed about where weaving was actually happening, Vishnu casually said:

"Sir, a lot of work is done on job-work basis with outside powerlooms; we only give yarn and get finished sarees back."

However, the job-work documentation was weak, and in some months, MKC had booked job-work movements as "sales" of yarn and "purchases" of fabric, artificially inflating turnover.

This is the same pattern often seen when borrowers try to "pump" top-line numbers to justify higher limits or make leverage look reasonable.

6.3 True Working Capital Requirement vs Proposed Limits

On paper, based on FY 2025-26 provisional figures submitted by the CA:

- Turnover: ₹18.50 crore.
- Debtors: ₹4.20 crore (83-85 days).
- Inventory: ₹3.00 crore (60 days).
- Creditors: ₹2.40 crore (47-50 days).

Assuming these numbers as-is, a conventional working capital assessment could superficially justify a CC limit of around ₹4-4.5 crore.

However, once the credit team excluded pseudo "job-work sales" and removed clearly circular related-party sales to Nair Ethnic Exports LLP and Nair Textiles Traders the estimated genuine external turnover dropped to ₹10-11 crore.

For Kasavu/fabric with a realistic net working capital cycle of 60-75 days, the true working capital requirement was recalculated at ₹2.0-2.5 crore.

In this scenario:

a) The existing ₹4.00 crore CC at Coastal State Bank itself appeared significantly higher than justified.

b) The requested enhancement to ₹4.50 crore, plus a fresh term loan of ₹1.50 crore, would mean serious over-funding relative to the real business base.

6.4 Stock, Creditors & Group Debtors - DP & Financial Manipulation

When MKC's stock statements submitted to Coastal State Bank were examined, several inconsistencies emerged:

a) In one month, MKC had declared stock of ₹7.80 crore and book-debts of ₹3.20 crore, with creditors of barely ₹90 lakh.

b) But the cumulative purchases as per GST for the preceding period were far lower than what would be required to support such stock, even after adding reasonable value addition.

c) The declared stock figure was simply not reconcilable with purchase volumes, margin structures, and creditor levels.

Further, it was observed that:

- Around 30-35% of outstanding debtors in the DP statements belonged to related entities (including Nair Ethnic Exports LLP).
- Both Coastal State Bank's sanction terms and KDB's internal credit policy explicitly disallow DP on group debtors / related parties.
- Despite this, these group debtors were being taken for DP and used to draw funds - a clear breach of both policy and prudent banking practice.

Also, in the unaudited financials for the previous year:

a) MKC had shown only ₹40 lakh closing stock while GST data indicated purchases exceeding ₹2.30 crore with negligible sales in that early period.

b) This pointed to "polished" financials - numbers adjusted to look lean and efficient, rather than reflecting actual inventory build-up.

Such manipulation of stock and creditor data is a direct integrity issue, not a mere documentation gap.

6.5 Diversion of Funds for Personal Villa & Security Substitution

The credit team carefully tracked capital and large-value movements from the CC account.

Over a 9-10 month period, MKC had withdrawn/paid out approximately ₹1.25 crore from the CC limit towards a builder/contractor for a luxury villa project near Fort Kochi, and Interior designer and premium fittings vendors.

When asked, Vishnu initially described it as:

"Some house renovation and family emergency needs."

However, subsequent market enquiries and site visit confirmed that this was a new high-end villa, not a basic renovation. The timing clearly showed that:

a) A major portion of this villa funding came from the working capital limit at Coastal State Bank.

b) Shortly after completing the villa, Vishnu proposed to offer it as collateral to KDB to "further strengthen" the security cover.

This is a classic pattern of fund diversion and post-facto security substitution, which fundamentally violates the spirit of working capital finance.

6.6 Integrity & Transparency Concerns - Family Default, Guarantees, Business Loans

The ROC/MCA checks revealed that:

a) Vishnu's father, Narayanan Nair, was a director in Kerala Heritage Silks Pvt. Ltd., which had significant unresolved MSME dues and multiple NPA accounts with various lenders.

b) While this did not automatically make Vishnu a defaulter, it raised important questions about the family's track record with bank funding.

When KDB requested Corporate guarantee from one of the stronger group entities handling gold jewellery trading, and CIBIL reports and full financials of the related textile and trading concerns (including Nair Ethnic Exports LLP and Nair Textiles Traders), Vishnu categorically refused:

"Sanction only in the name of Malabar Kasavu Creations. Group guarantees are not required. If you are not comfortable, we will continue with our existing bankers."

Separately, CIBIL and statement analysis also showed:

a) Vishnu had raised around ₹80-90 lakh of unsecured business loans over the last 18 months from NBFCs and fintech lenders.

b) Some of these were under credit guarantee / CGTMSE-type schemes via his small proprietorship concern.

c) These loans, at high effective interest rates, had been regularly rolled over or refinanced, reflecting structural liquidity stress, not temporary mismatch.

A promoter who:

a) Inflates stock and DP,

b) Diverts bank funds to build a luxury villa,

c) Refuses group guarantee and full financial transparency, and

d) Heavily relies on expensive BLs to plug cash-flow gaps

cannot be given the same risk weight as a clean, transparent SME.

6.7 Dual Banking, Routing Pattern & Site Visit Findings

Under RBI's guidelines on current accounts and CC/OD accounts, borrowers are expected to:

- Route the bulk of their operational transactions through the main working capital banker, and
- Avoid multiple current accounts without proper NOC and regulatory compliance.

In MKC's case, the pattern was worrying:

a) Although Coastal State Bank was the primary CC banker, substantial churning was happening in a current account with South Coast Bank, and a current account recently opened with Kerala Development Bank itself.

b) Transfers between these accounts were often round-figured and did not always correlate clearly with documented sales and purchases.

This dual-banking pattern is a classic red flag: it allows the borrower to keep lenders in the dark about the true level of business and cash flows.

The unit visit made things worse:

a) The factory floor had far fewer looms running than claimed; on a weekday afternoon, only a portion of machines were operating.

b) Finished saree stock in the warehouse was much lower than what would be expected for a business claiming ₹18+ crore turnover.

c) Many sarees on racks seemed old designs, with dust and faded tags – suggesting slow movement.

d) The retail showroom was aesthetically pleasing but had limited footfall during the visit; staff admitted that a sizeable portion of displayed stock technically belonged to weavers on consignment basis, and not to MKC.

When confronted with these discrepancies, Vishnu's explanations shifted between:

- *"Season is just over, that is why stock is low."*
- *"We have moved goods to godowns near Thrissur,"* but no clear documentation.

The disconnect between on-ground operations and on-paper figures seriously undermined the credibility of the entire proposal.

7. Outcome / Final Decision

After consolidating the above findings, the Credit Team prepared a comprehensive note for the Zonal Credit Committee of Kerala Development Bank.

Key conclusions were:

a) A large portion of turnover appeared to be engineered through round-tripping with related parties, job-work misclassification, and circular routing.

b) Working capital assessment, when based on realistic external sales and reasonable cycle, showed that existing limits at Coastal State Bank were already more than adequate; enhancement plus fresh TL at KDB would amount to over-funding.

c) There was clear evidence of fund diversion from working capital limits for constructing a personal villa, later "offered" as security - indicating poor credit discipline and weak respect for end-use.

d) Stock, creditors and debtors data were not reliable; DP statements to the existing bank were inflated and non-compliant, including ineligible group debtors.

e) The promoter's behaviour - refusal to give group guarantees, non-sharing of full group financials, and aggressive posturing ("sanction on what you have or we will not proceed") - was not aligned with what KDB expects from a borrower seeking multi-crore limits.

f) Family background showed linkage with earlier large defaults in the textile segment, adding to the integrity risk.

g) Dual banking and weak site visit findings strengthened the view that this was not a case of "documentation gaps" but of fundamental intent and integrity risk.

Accordingly, the Committee decided:

- Not to take over the existing facilities from Coastal State Bank.
- Not to sanction any fresh working capital or term loan to MKC.
- To politely decline the proposal, documenting the reasons in detail and flagging the case internally as a "high integrity risk" profile for future reference.

The branch was advised to continue only with non-fund, low-risk banking services (savings, deposits, simple current account with strict monitoring) if at all, but no fund-based credit exposure.

8. Key Lessons for Credit Professionals

a) Never accept seasonal turnover at face value - always align banking data with the natural business cycle and GST/HSN profile.

b) Recalculate working capital needs on realistic external sales and credible cycles; over-funding is a breeding ground for diversion and future NPAs.

c) Treat inflated stock, understated creditors, and inclusion of group debtors in DP as integrity issues, not mere technical discrepancies.

d) Track capital withdrawals and large transfers from CC accounts - repeated use of WC limits to build personal assets is a serious violation of end-use.

f) Promoter transparency, willingness to share group data, and readiness to give corporate guarantees often tell you more than audited financials.

g) Multiple high-cost business loans and dual banking patterns signal structural stress and weak intent, even when CIBIL and collateral look good.

h) Unit visits are non-negotiable in borderline cases - if ground reality doesn't match the story in the files, trust what you see, not what you are told.

i) A disciplined credit officer must be ready to say "NO" to attractive-looking, fully collateralised proposals when integrity, data quality and end-use risks are fundamentally unacceptable.

•••

CASE STUDY 22

THE SOLVENCY CERTIFICATE THAT CARRIED MORE RISK THAN THE LOAN ITSELF

How misunderstanding the nature of unconditional guarantees sealed the loss

1. Introduction

Non-fund based facilities are often treated casually in branches because no money actually goes out. In reality, a single poorly structured Bank Guarantee (BG) or Deferred Payment Guarantee (DPG) can convert into a full-blown funded exposure overnight and wipe out years of branch profit.

This case study traces how a mid-sized EPC(Engineering, Procurement, and Construction) contractor's government road project, backed by a seemingly modest non-fund limit of ₹78 lakh, turned into an expensive lesson for a public-sector bank. The case highlights gaps in solvency certificate issuance, BG structuring, operational discipline, and invocation handling.

2. Borrower / Business Background

Borrower: Vertex Infra Projects Pvt Ltd (VIPL).

Nature of business: EPC contractor specialising in small to mid-size road and drainage projects for State PWD and Municipal Corporations.

Constitution: Private Limited Company, in existence for 8 years.

Turnover: Around ₹24-26 crore in the last two years, largely from government contracts.

Banking: Main banking with National Trust Bank (NTB), Guntur Branch, for the last 5 years with: a) Cash Credit of ₹3 crore (secured by stock, book debts and collateral EM on residential property). b) Occasional ad-hoc BGs for earnest money and performance, all honoured in the past.

3. Sanctioned Non-Fund Facility

Recently, VIPL won a tender from Guntur Municipal Corporation (GMC) for widening and strengthening a 14-km ring road, contract value around ₹18 crore. As per tender and contract, the following banking support was needed:

Performance BG: 5% of contract value - ₹60 lakh.

Deferred Payment Guarantee: ₹18 lakh to cover mobilisation advance adjustment over 18 months.

NTB sanctioned a composite non-fund based facility of ₹78 lakh in favour of GMC with the following broad terms:

a) 20% cash margin for BGs to be kept in fixed deposit.
b) Collateral already charged for CC (residential property, estimated value ₹3.2 crore) to secure the non-fund exposure as well.
c) Standard IBA-based BG format with clear expiry and claim period.
d) All BGs to be issued through SFMS(Structured Financial Messaging System) to the beneficiary's banker.

Theoretically, the structure appeared conservative but the real problems started before the BG was issued.

4. Pre-Sanction Trigger - The Solvency Certificate

GMC required a Solvency Certificate of ₹3 crore from VIPL's banker as part of tender eligibility. The borrower approached the Branch Manager (BM) of NTB, Ms. Ananya Rao, in a hurry because the last date for tender submission was the next day.

The Relationship Manager (RM) argued that:

a) VIPL had a long banking relationship with timely servicing of CC.
b) Existing limits and collateral value "indirectly" indicated capacity.
c) Other banks "routinely" issued such certificates for good clients.

Without a detailed financial analysis of VIPL's net worth or outside liabilities, the BM signed a solvency certificate for ₹3 crore, largely based on past conduct and collateral estimates. The certificate contained a general disclaimer but, in GMC's eyes, it acted as an implicit endorsement of VIPL's financial strength.

GMC accepted the tender and awarded the contract to VIPL. The bank's perceived support, via this certificate, had played a key role.

5. Key Developments

5.1 Issuance of Performance BG and DPG

After receiving the Letter of Acceptance from GMC, VIPL requested issuance of:

- Performance BG of ₹60 lakh.
- DPG of ₹18 lakh for mobilisation advance.

Due to time pressure, the branch:

a) Released the Performance BG using an older Word template lying on the branch system, not the latest vetted IBA format.

b) Collected only 10% cash margin instead of 20%, citing relationship and tight borrower liquidity.

c) Did not modify the BG to include a strong "Notwithstanding" clause clearly specifying the maximum liability, expiry date and limited claim period; instead, the wording was generic and allowed GMC to invoke the full amount "at any time during the contract or till obligations are fulfilled".

d) Issued the BG manually first and sent the SFMS message to GMC's banker the next day; details matched, but the manual hard copy was treated as the primary instrument by GMC.

The DPG was also issued with similar relaxed margin (10%) and without clearly capturing the schedule of reduction linked to work progress bills.

5.2 Project Delays and Early Warning Signals

Within 6 months, multiple stress signals emerged:

a) Land acquisition and utility shifting were delayed by the local authorities.

b) VIPL had to demobilise and remobilise equipment multiple times, causing cost overrun.

c) CC account started showing frequent overdrawings, with TODs approved on verbal assurances.

d) Statutory dues such as GST were unpaid for two quarters; Audit trail for subcontractor payments weakened.

Despite these signs, the branch considered the risk "manageable" because:

- No instalments were due under funded limits.
- BGs and DPG were only non-fund based, assumed to be low-risk unless invoked.

Credit monitoring focused on CC turnover and stock statements; no specific review of BG exposure or the project's physical progress was done.

5.3 Termination of Contract and Invocation Notice

After repeated extensions and warnings, GMC terminated the contract at around 40% completion, citing:

- Failure to meet milestones.
- Quality deficiencies in drainage works.
- Non-payment to some local subcontractors, leading to site disruptions.

Within a week, GMC sent:

- Invocation of Performance BG for full ₹60 lakh, stating breach of contractual obligations.
- Demand under DPG for ₹12 lakh, being the unadjusted portion of mobilisation advance.

The invocation letter reached NTB's branch and its email copy reached the regional office. It was received within the BG validity period, clearly quoting BG numbers, amount and referencing the underlying contract.

The branch was now staring at an immediate liquidity outgo of ₹72 lakh (₹60 lakh + ₹12 lakh) against a non-fund limit of ₹78 lakh.

6. Problem Statement

a) Solvency certificate issued without robust financial verification, indirectly enabling the borrower to win a large contract beyond its genuine financial capacity.

b) Bank Guarantees and DPG structured and issued with deviations from sanctioned terms and best-practice formats (lower margin, non-standard wording, weak limitation/claim period).

c) Inadequate post-issuance monitoring of project performance and BG exposure, despite clear early warning signals in both operations and borrower behaviour.

d) Delayed and indecisive response to invocation, leading to full payout, stressed relationship with beneficiary, and a complex recovery situation from the borrower.

7. Detailed Analysis

7.1 Solvency Certificate - A Silent Risk Amplifier

A solvency certificate is not a guarantee, but in government tenders it often acts as a moral assurance from the banker about the contractor's financial strength. In VIPL's case:

a) The certificate amount of ₹3 crore was far higher than the bank's assessed drawing power or promoter's tangible net worth.

b) No fresh financial statements, income-tax returns or external credit reports were obtained before issuing it.

c) The disclaimer "without any liability on the bank" was included, but the BM did not limit the certificate to "based on conduct of account and securities held" or cap it to verified net worth.

As a result, the bank indirectly facilitated the award of a contract that was too large for the contractor's balance sheet, increasing the chance that BGs would eventually be invoked. From a credit-culture angle, the BM treated the solvency certificate as a mere service item, not as a quasi-risk instrument which should be rooted in hard data and subject to policy limits.

7.2 Structuring and Issuance of BG / DPG - Deviations with Hidden Consequences

The sanctioned terms clearly prescribed 20% margin and standard vetted formats. However, in practice:

a) Margin was reduced to 10% purely to "help the client mobilise machinery".

b) The BG wording did not strictly cap liability or set a short claim period after expiry. A broad, unconditional guarantee was issued which allowed GMC to invoke any time during the contract until obligations were fully performed.

c) The DPG schedule of reduction was not properly documented; only a general clause was inserted that "guarantee amount shall reduce in proportion to completion of work", leaving scope for dispute.

These deviations had three critical effects:

a) **Economic risk:** With only 10% margin, the bank's unsecured exposure on invocation increased materially.

b) **Legal risk:** Non-standard wording significantly strengthened the beneficiary's position and reduced the bank's ability to contest invocation.

c) **Operational risk:** The absence of a clear DPG reduction schedule made it difficult to prove what portion of mobilisation advance had been adjusted.

In hindsight, the branch effectively underpriced and under-secured a high-risk non-fund exposure.

7.3 Monitoring Failure - Treating Non-Fund Limits as Dormant

Throughout the project duration, the branch did not:

a) Call for periodic project progress reports or copies of running bills certified by the engineer-in-charge.

b) Track cumulative billed percentage via original contract milestones.

c) Reassess whether BG value needed reduction as work progressed.

d) Flag CIBIL changes, statutory overdues, and subcontractor complaints as red flags linked to BG invocation risk.

The RM believed that since VIPL had "never defaulted", the BGs were safe. In reality, multiple stress points like delayed government payments, stretched CC account, rising outside borrowing, tax arrears were classic early-warning signals.

An early intervention (for example, insisting on enhanced margin, partial reduction of BG in line with progress, or even advising the borrower to exit the project) could have mitigated the impact.

7.4 Handling of Invocation - Obligation vs Relationship

On receipt of GMC's invocation letter, the branch reacted defensively:

a) RM immediately contacted VIPL, who claimed that termination was "arbitrary" and that they planned to litigate.

b) VIPL requested the bank to "hold payment" until they obtained a stay order.

c) The branch attempted to negotiate informally with GMC officials for "some more time", citing the contractor's difficulties.

However, the guarantee was unconditional. There was:

- Clear reference to BG and contract numbers.
- Invocation within validity period.
- Demand for payment of specified sum to GMC's designated bank account.

Head Office Legal Cell categorically advised that, as per guarantee wording and prevailing legal principles, NTB had no option but to honour the invocation immediately, except if a competent court granted a stay or if there was clear evidence of fraud by the beneficiary, neither of which existed.

NTB therefore:

- Paid ₹60 lakh under Performance BG and ₹12 lakh under DPG, within 48 hours, through RTGS to GMC's banker.
- Converted the non-fund exposure into a funded demand loan in VIPL's name.
- Adjusted the 10% margin FD and marked the residual as overdue.

Within six months, VIPL could not regularise the liability; CC account also turned irregular. The entire exposure was eventually classified as NPA.

7.5 Recovery and Accountability

The bank initiated multiple actions:

a) Invoked the personal guarantees of directors and issued recall notices.
b) Registered equitable mortgage charge and started SARFAESI proceedings on the residential property; partial recovery was achieved after two years through sale.
c) Balance shortfall remained, necessitating full provisioning.

An internal investigation found:

a) BM had breached delegated authority by diluting margin without prior sanction modification.
b) Non-standard guarantee format was used without Head Office approval.
c) Solvency certificate was issued without documented financial analysis.
d) Absence of documented post-issuance review of BG exposure, despite clear stress indicators such as CC overdrawings, GST arrears, and project delays.

As a result:

a) BM received a major penalty and was shifted out of credit role.

b) RM received a warning letter for poor monitoring and non-detection of early warning signals.

c) The branch implemented stricter controls on non-fund limits and started routing all high-value BGs through regional credit cell.

d) Policy-level clarification was issued treating high-value solvency certificates and performance guarantees as credit substitutes, requiring credit approval, documented financial justification, and maker-checker accountability similar to funded limits.

8. Key Lessons for Credit Professionals

a) **Treat solvency certificates as risk-sensitive instruments, not mere service letters.** Always base the amount on verified financial data, recorded securities, and documented analysis; avoid issuing high-value certificates only on relationship comfort.

b) **Never dilute sanctioned terms on margin, security, or format for convenience.** Any change in BG or DPG structure must be formally approved and documented; non-standard wording can drastically increase the bank's legal and economic liability.

c) **Monitor non-fund based facilities with the same seriousness as funded limits.** Track project progress, running bills, disputes, and external red flags; where performance is slipping, consider seeking additional margin, reducing guarantee value or advising client to de-risk.

d) **Ensure robust operational discipline in issuance of guarantees.** Use only approved formats, issue BGs strictly through SFMS, obtain client's signed counter-guarantee, and maintain complete records including three copies and acknowledgement from the beneficiary.

e) **On invocation, focus first on the bank's obligation, then on borrower relationship.** If invocation is compliant with guarantee terms and within validity, honour promptly and separately pursue recovery from the borrower; delaying payment to "help" the client can expose the bank to legal and reputational risk.

f) **Embed accountability and learning in branch credit culture.** Every large loss case must be analysed for process gaps like sanction deviations, monitoring failures, documentation lapses and converted into practical checklists and training inputs so that future non-fund limits are handled with far greater rigour.

•••

CASE STUDY 23

PARI PASSU GONE WRONG: A ₹56 CRORE STEEL CONSORTIUM AND THE BATTLE FOR THE SAME SECURITY

1. Introduction

When a promising mid-sized steel manufacturer in Raipur, Chhattisgarh defaulted on a ₹56 crore consortium facility, the immediate question for the lenders was not whether the account was NPA. The real fight began later i.e. who would get how much from sale of the same factory, and where the newly added "second pari passu" lenders stood in the recovery waterfall.

This case traces the journey of a seemingly well-structured consortium, the creation of pari passu and second pari passu charges, and the painful lessons that followed when enforcement under SARFAESI exposed gaps in understanding, documentation and registration of charges.

2. Borrower & Business Background

Chhattisgarh Alloy Steels Private Limited (CASPL) was a 12-year-old steel rolling mill located in the Raipur Industrial Cluster of Chhattisgarh. The company manufactured MS (Mild Steel) billets and TMT bars used in construction and infrastructure projects.

Turnover had grown from ₹220 crore to ₹270 crore in three years, but margins were thin and volatile, driven by raw-material prices and power costs. The business was capital-intensive, with a long operating cycle due to stocking of scrap and finished goods.

Promoters were first-generation entrepreneurs. They were aggressive on expansion, comfortable with leverage and often relied on short-term borrowing to plug cash-flow gaps.

3. Banking Arrangement & Facility Structure

Initially, Pratham Bank (lead bank) financed the company with a term loan and working capital limits. As sales increased, CASPL approached two more lenders and a three–bank consortium was formed.

As of FY 2024-25, the sanctioned consortium limits were:

a) **Pratham Bank (Lead Bank):**

Term Loan I & II: ₹15 crore

Cash Credit: ₹7 crore

Non-fund based limits (LC/BG): ₹4 crore

Total exposure: ₹26 crore

b) **Navchetan Bank:**

Term Loan: ₹10 crore

Cash Credit: ₹6 crore

LC/BG: ₹2 crore

Total exposure: ₹18 crore

c) **Sahaj Development Bank:**

Cash Credit: ₹8 crore

LC/BG: ₹4 crore

Total exposure: ₹12 crore

Total consortium facilities: ₹56 crore.

All three lenders agreed to share a pari passu first charge on:

- Land and building of the plant
- Plant and machinery
- Entire current assets (stocks and receivables)

Personal guarantees of promoters and a corporate guarantee of an associate company supported the facilities. An Inter-Creditor Agreement (ICA) captured the sharing of security and laid down that in the event of enforcement, realizations from the charged assets would be shared in proportion to the outstanding dues of each bank on the date of distribution.

4. Understanding the Pari Passu Structure

During appraisal, the lead bank's credit department circulated an internal note to all consortium members to align understanding of pari passu sharing.

It explained that when multiple lenders hold a pari passu charge, they share sale proceeds proportionate to their respective outstanding, not equally by headcount. For illustration, it gave an example:

If Bank X and Bank Y together lend ₹100 crore in the ratio 60:40 and there is common security worth ₹50 crore, both having pari passu first charge, then on enforcement Bank X will receive ₹30 crore and Bank Y will receive ₹20 crore from that asset.

The note also clarified that if additional lenders subsequently take a second pari passu charge on the same asset, those lenders will be entitled to share in the realizations only after the dues of the first pari passu charge holders are fully satisfied, and then in proportion to their respective outstanding.

Conceptually, all lenders acknowledged this framework. In practice, however, not everyone embedded it into their risk pricing, loan conditions, and monitoring mechanisms.

5. Entry of Second Pari Passu Lenders

In FY 2025-26, CASPL faced margin pressure due to a sudden fall in finished steel prices and a spike in power tariffs. The company's internal accruals were inadequate to service term loans and fund increased working capital needs.

The consortium resisted further enhancement without fresh equity. Promoters, keen to complete a capacity upgradation project, approached two systemically important NBFCs: Aarohan Capital Finance Ltd and Growthridge Finance Ltd.

These NBFCs sanctioned the following facilities:

- Aarohan Capital: Term Loan of ₹3 crore
- Growthridge Finance: Term Loan of ₹3 crore

Both facilities were sanctioned against a "second pari passu charge" on the same land, building and plant & machinery already charged to the consortium.

Key weaknesses emerged:

a) **Inadequate consent process:**
   - Pratham Bank issued a conditional NOC permitting second charge up to ₹6 crore.
   - Navchetan Bank and Sahaj Gramin Bank did not formally approve the detailed term sheets; only a generic board resolution existed allowing secondary charges subject to security cover.

b) **Imperfect registration:**

- The NBFCs created charge at ROC and CERSAI. While their loan documents clearly mentioned "second charge", one of the CERSAI entries erroneously ticked "pari passu" without specifying subordination.
- The consortium banks did not verify or insist on rectification.

c) **ICA not updated:** The original ICA between the three banks was never amended to record the presence and rights of second charge lenders.

At this stage, total secured borrowing against the core fixed assets reached ₹62 crore (₹56 crore first pari passu + ₹6 crore second pari passu), while the latest valuation of those assets stood at around ₹45 crore on a realistic basis.

6. Deterioration & Default

Over the next 12 months, CASPL's position worsened:

a) Sales volumes dipped as infrastructure projects slowed.

b) Debtors stretched their payment cycles beyond 120 days.

c) LC devolvements and BG invocations started hitting the cash credit limits.

d) Interest on term loans was irregular and accounts slipped from SMA-0 to SMA-1 and then SMA-2.

Despite restructuring discussions, promoters could not infuse equity or bring in a strategic investor. All three consortium banks classified the account as NPA.

Outstanding fund-based exposures at the time of NPA were approximately:

Pratham Bank: ₹24 crore.

Navchetan Bank: ₹18 crore.

Sahaj Gramin Bank: ₹10 crore.

The two NBFCs each had an outstanding of about ₹3 crore.

With no credible revival plan, the consortium decided to enforce security under the SARFAESI Act, 2002. Pratham Bank, as lead bank, issued notice under Section 13(2) and later took symbolic possession under Section 13(4), acting on behalf of all first charge lenders.

7. Enforcement and the Dispute

The plant and machinery, along with land and building, were put to auction through the SARFAESI process. After two failed attempts, the assets were finally sold for ₹38 crore. A further ₹4 crore was realized from receivables and scrap sale, taking total realizations from secured assets to ₹42 crore.

When it came to distribution of sale proceeds, two disputes arose:

a) Among first pari passu lenders themselves, there was clarity that sharing should be in proportion to outstanding dues. Based on total first charge outstanding of ₹52 crore (24 + 18 + 10), their shares in the ₹42 crore realization worked out to roughly:

   Pratham Bank: about ₹19.38 crore

   Navchetan Bank: about ₹14.54 crore

   Sahaj Gramin Bank: about ₹8.08 crore

b) Second pari passu lenders claimed equal priority.

   - Aarohan and Growthridge argued that because one of the CERSAI entries mentioned "pari passu" without the word "second", they should participate in the same pool of realizations along with the three banks.
   - They also contended that the generic board resolution and earlier correspondence from the banks amounted to consent for pari passu sharing, not merely second charge.

The consortium banks relied on their sanction terms and legal opinion that:

a) Loan documents of the NBFCs clearly referred to second charge,

b) The NOC issued by Pratham Bank explicitly used the phrase "subservient / second charge",

c) ICA never granted equal ranking to the NBFCs,

d) And under SARFAESI, distribution should follow the documented priority of charges, not merely the CERSAI tick-box.

The matter escalated to the Debts Recovery Tribunal (DRT), causing a delay of more than a year in final appropriation of sale proceeds.

8. Detailed Analysis & Discussion

From a credit-risk perspective, several structural weaknesses become clear.

8.1 Security Cover and Leverage

At the time second charge loans were sanctioned, total borrowing against core fixed assets had already reached a level where realizable value (about ₹45 crore) was lower than the aggregate first pari passu exposure (₹56 crore).

By allowing an additional second charge of ₹6 crore without insisting on fresh collateral or equity, the system effectively converted an already tight security position into a significantly under-secured one.

A prudent approach would have been:

a) To restrict further borrowing to separate collateral, or

b) To insist that any new lender join the existing pari passu pool with full re-assessment and revised ICA, or

c) To decline additional leverage altogether.

8.2 Documentation and Inter-Creditor Arrangements

The ICA described pari passu sharing among the three banks but was silent on the possibility of new lenders obtaining second charges. It also did not contain explicit covenants preventing the borrower from creating further charges without unanimous lender consent.

RBI's guidance on consortium and multiple banking arrangements stresses the need for clear inter-creditor agreements, information sharing and due diligence through CERSAI/ROC searches. Failure to update the ICA when second charge lenders entered effectively left a grey zone which later became a litigation hotspot.

8.3 Charge Registration and CERSAI

Under the SARFAESI regime, creation of security interest on immovable and movable properties must be registered with CERSAI and ROC to be enforceable against third parties. The rules also provide that where multiple lenders are secured on the same asset, priority and whether the charge is pari passu or subordinate should be clearly recorded.

In this case, one NBFC's charge was recorded on CERSAI as "pari passu" without marking it as second. This clerical error, left unchecked, gave the NBFC a foothold to argue equal ranking. Though DRT ultimately upheld the banks' claim based on underlying loan documents and NOC wording, the mistake prolonged litigation and weakened the banks' negotiating position.

8.4 Recovery under SARFAESI vs. IBC

The consortium chose SARFAESI enforcement instead of immediately moving under the Insolvency and Bankruptcy Code (IBC). Under IBC, Section 53 of the Code prescribes a waterfall for distribution in liquidation, and recent NCLT jurisprudence has generally respected contractually agreed priorities between first and second charge holders.

In SARFAESI enforcement, too, distribution follows documented priorities. However, absence of a single, binding resolution plan meant that each secured creditor looked at recovery from a narrow, bank-specific lens. The NBFCs, not being part of the ICA, were outside the consortium coordination mechanism and therefore pursued an aggressive legal strategy, including challenging the lead bank's right to distribute proceeds without their consent.

8.5 Provisioning and Capital Impact

Due to the prolonged dispute, the three banks could not fully appropriate the entire ₹42 crore for over a year. During this period, RBI's prudential norms required them to maintain higher provisioning on the outstanding NPA, adversely impacting profitability and capital adequacy.

Had the charges, ICA and CERSAI records been crystal clear from day one, the same sale proceeds could have been appropriated, residual exposure quantified quickly, and the banks could have taken timely calls on technical write-offs or further recovery measures.

9. Outcome / Final Decision

After multiple hearings, the DRT held that:

a) Loan documentation, sanction letters and NOC clearly established first pari passu charge of the three banks and second charge of the two NBFCs on the plant and machinery and land & building.

b) The erroneous CERSAI entry could not, by itself, override the explicit contractual terms between borrower and lenders.

Accordingly, the Tribunal directed that:

a) The entire ₹42 crore realization from secured assets be distributed among the three first charge lenders in proportion to their outstanding dues.
b) Second charge lenders, Aarohan and Growthridge, would have rights only over any surplus from the same assets after satisfying first charge dues (which, in this case, did not arise) and over any other unencumbered assets or guarantor properties.

Post-distribution, the banks' residual exposures were:

Pratham Bank: about ₹4.62 crore.

Navchetan Bank: about ₹3.46 crore.

Sahaj Gramin Bank: about ₹1.92 crore.

These balances were pursued through recovery from guarantors and other legal avenues, with partial success. The account ultimately resulted in significant write-offs for all lenders, and almost full loss for the two NBFCs.

10. Key Lessons for Credit Professionals

a) Pari passu means equal ranking, not equal recovery. Always compute your bank's expected share of realizable security value based on pro-rata outstanding, not headcount of lenders.
b) Before permitting any second or additional charge on core securities, re-assess total leverage, realistic valuations and whether incremental borrowing is justified by cash flows and risk appetite.
c) Treat inter-creditor agreements as living documents, update them whenever new lenders join, limits change or security is re-allocated, and ensure all lenders explicitly agree to the revised sharing.
d) Regularly review ROC and CERSAI records to ensure that type of charge (first, second, pari passu, subordinate) and inter-se priorities are correctly captured; rectify any discrepancy immediately with legal support.
e) At the first signs of stress, align all secured creditors on a common recovery strategy, including choice between SARFAESI and IBC, to avoid fragmented action and later disputes over enforcement and distribution.

f) Price and structure consortium exposures realistically. Do not treat pari passu security on a heavily leveraged asset as equivalent to an exclusive first charge; build in higher pricing, tighter conditions or demand additional collateral to compensate for structural subordination risk.

•••

ABOUT THE AUTHOR

Kumar Gaurav Khullar is a seasoned banker, trade finance expert, and educator with rich, hands-on experience across urban and rural branch banking. An ex-banker with Bank of India and Punjab & Sind Bank, he has worked extensively in General Banking, Credit/Advances, and Risk Management, bringing real operational clarity to complex banking concepts.

He holds an MBA from the Indian Institute of Management, Raipur (IIM Raipur) and a Master of Computer Applications (MCA) from the Centre for Development of Advanced Computing (CDAC, Noida). He is also JAIIB and CAIIB certified by the Indian Institute of Banking and Finance (IIBF), along with specialised certifications from NIBSCOM (National Institute of Banking Studies & Corporate Management) and other premier institutions.

In 2018, he transitioned from banking to teaching and content creation with a clear mission: to simplify banking and finance for working professionals and make certification journeys more structured, practical, and achievable. Since then, he has guided countless bankers and finance professionals in preparing for JAIIB, CAIIB, Certified Credit Professional (CCP), Anti-Money Laundering (AML), and Trade Finance examinations.

A popular instructor, he teaches best-selling courses on Udemy, including the Basel Norms Masterclass and Incoterms 2020 Masterclass, known for their clarity and strong student feedback. He also runs a specialised, case-study-driven Bank Financial Management programme designed for bankers and finance professionals.

His first book, *The Fearless Banker*, bridges the gap between textbook learning and real-world banking. Built on years of practical experience, it features 39 caselets based on situations bankers commonly face, offering ethical, efficient, and actionable decision frameworks. His second book, *Bank Promotion Interview Secrets*, supports bankers and NBFC professionals with practical mock interviews and interview-ready preparation.

He also leads a YouTube community of 55,000+ learners, where he shares practical insights on banking, career growth, and professional survival strategies. His sessions on topics such as factoring and forfeiting, taking charge of a new branch, loan proposals, documentation, NPA prevention, and vigilance awareness have helped thousands of bankers navigate day-to-day challenges with confidence.

Driven by a mission to empower bankers with knowledge and professional judgement, Kumar Gaurav Khullar continues to bridge theory and practice through his books, courses, and mentoring, helping professionals not only clear exams, but also build stronger careers in banking.

You can contact the Author at –

kumargauravkhullar1@gmail.com
Ph-7830481000 (WhatsApp)

www.ingramcontent.com/pod-product-compliance
Lightning Source LLC
LaVergne TN
LVHW100307210926
848480LV00003B/1051